TURNING POINTS IN HISTORY

STATESMEN

WHO CHANGED THE WORLD

Philip Wilkinson & Jacqueline Dineen

Illustrations by Robert Ingpen

DRAGON'S
WORLD

CHILDREN'S
BOOKS

Dragon's World Ltd
Limpsfield
Surrey RH8 0DY
Great Britain

First published by Dragon's World 1994

Simplified text and captions by **Jacqueline Dineen**
based on the *Encyclopedia of World Events*
by Robert Ingpen & Philip Wilkinson

Editor	Diana Briscoe
Project Editor	Paul Bennett
Designer	Design 23
Art Director	John Strange
Design Assistant	Victoria Furbisher
DTP Manager	Keith Bambury
Editorial Director	Pippa Rubinstein

**British Library Cataloguing
in Publication Data**
The catalogue record for this book
is available from the British Library.

ISBN 1 85028 234 X

Typeset in New Baskerville, Swiss and Fenice by Dragon's World Ltd.
Printed in Italy

Contents

Introduction

A statesman (or woman) is a person who moves with confidence and influence around the world, not just in their own country. Their decisions have a impact further afield than just their own country. The greatest statesmen of all are those whose actions have transformed the world. Sometimes this is achieved by peaceful means, and sometimes on the battlefield. But there is usually some master plan, involving the destinies of nations or empires.

A truly great statesman has a vision of the way in which he or she wants to change the world. The great Indian ruler, Asoka,

for example, was the first to unite India. It needed great political and military strength, but it was powered by Asoka's desire to convert all of India to Buddhism. Great empires have been built on a vision of an equal society. Lenin and the Bolsheviks built the USSR inspired by communism, and Mao Zedong united the warring regions of China behind the same banner. Matching the vision to the time, place and people is vital – Mao

Julius Caesar's rule saw power transferred from the Roman Senate to the Emperors who followed him

China was first united under Shih Huang Ti

Civilizations collided when Cortés found the Aztec Empire

221 BC

44 BC

1521

had the ideal brand of communism for people who mostly lived by farming.

Perhaps the most admirable statesmen are those who have stood up for the oppressed. Simón Bolívar campaigned across South America to free the Spanish colonies from the inefficient rule of the Viceroys. More recently, Gandhi was the inspirational leader who led non-violent resistance to British rule in India. Eleanor Roosevelt persuaded politicians in 1946 to create the United Nations Organization and to define the basic rights of all humans in its Charter.

Today statesmen are desperately needed in the aftermath of the fall of the Berlin Wall. Old national disputes have reappeared with the collapse of various communist regimes. Across the world, many politicians are working on solutions which will make the world a better place in the future.

Philip Wilkinson

Lenin and the Bolsheviks founded the first communist state

The United Nations was founded to prevent another world war

Gandhi's non-violent campaigns won independence for India

The fall of the Berlin Wall opened a new era in Europe

1917   1930   1946   1989

Asoka, the Buddhist Emperor

Asoka wanted Kalinga – it was the last bit of India out of his control. He sent his armies to conquer it, but the slaughter that followed revolted him so much that he turned to Buddhism, a religion that values life. For the rest of his life he encouraged his subjects to live in harmony with each other, and made laws to promote this goal.

| 400 | | BC/AD | | 400 | | 800 | | 1200 | | 1600 | | 2000 |

c.250 BC Pataliputra, India

The civilization of India is one of the oldest in the world. However, the people who settled there were not united under one ruler until the reign of the Mauryan emperor, Asoka, who came to the throne in 272 BC.

happened in the area for the next 1000 years. Then towns and cities began to grow up on the plain of the Ganges river. Northern India was divided into separate states, which eventually united into one state, Magadha.

Flourishing civilization disappears

Farming communities had begun to settle in the Indus Valley, in what is now Pakistan, in about 6000 BC. By about 2500 BC, several cities had been built and a flourishing civilization was growing up around them. The greatest of these cities were Harappa and Mohenjo-daro, where a sophisticated culture developed. Then, in about 1750 BC, the two cities were abandoned and the Indus civilization disappeared.

Historians believe there must have been an invasion, but little is known about the end of this culture or what

Asoka, emperor of India (270–32 BC). He was the grandson of Chandragupta Maurya, founder of the Mauryan empire, and became the first person to rule the whole of India.

Invading Greeks

In 327 BC, Alexander the Great (356–323 BC) of Greece and his army swept across India, adding new lands to his mighty empire. After five years of fighting, however, his soldiers refused to continue and Alexander decided to return home. He left Greek governors in the parts of India he had conquered, but it was not long before they too went home.

Powerful dynasty

The way was now clear for a new and powerful dynasty to take over. Chandragupta Maurya came to the throne of Magadha in 321 BC, and began his conquest of the lands left by the Greeks. When he died in 297 BC, he had a large empire to hand over to his son, Bindusara.

The new king carried on his father's work and by the time he died in 272 BC, there was only one part of India which was not part of the Mauryan empire. This was Kalinga, on the east coast of the Bay of Bengal. Bindusara's son, Asoka, succeeded him and set out immediately to conquer Kalinga – so he became the first person to rule over the whole area which is now India.

Turning point

The reign of Asoka marks a turning point in history for two reasons. One is the way in which he ruled his large empire. The other is that he was so horrified by the bloodshed during his conquest of Kalinga that he turned his back on violence and converted to the Buddhist religion.

Asoka governed the empire from Pataliputra, a city on the Ganges. He set up trading links with neighbouring lands and built a network of roads for merchants to travel along. He also established an efficient form of government which allowed him to keep control over his people.

The central government consisted of a council of ministers who advised him and discussed policies – planned courses of action – with him. Other officials were based in different parts of the empire. Their job was to report back to the central government and also to collect taxes. They had a staff of junior officials which formed local governments throughout the empire.

When Asoka came to the throne, there were several different religions

in India. Asoka wanted to unite his people and teach them a non-violent way of life. He did this by helping and encouraging the spread of Buddhism throughout his empire.

The first Buddhists

Buddhism had been founded by Gautama Siddhartha (c. 563–c. 483 BC), but until the reign of Asoka, its followers were scattered across India in small groups. They were looking for personal enlightenment (spiritual truth) and not trying to convert new followers or organize themselves into one religion with a common aim.

This all changed when Buddhists came together at a famous meeting called the Third Council in about 250 BC. The people who attended it decided to send missionaries throughout the empire and beyond to teach people about Buddhism – the religion was to be spread far and wide.

Asoka's beliefs about how the king and his people should behave and the laws he made were engraved on rocks and pillars in prominent places throughout India. The inscriptions encouraged people to live a good life and find happiness by giving up bad ways such as cruelty and laziness.

Asoka's people began to see him as a wise teacher who could help them to reach heaven. Though he encouraged Buddhism, Asoka wanted to give people something they could all believe in, whatever their religion. This in turn would help him to keep

The peaceful face of Buddha is an important symbol in India. Though Indian Buddhism lost some influence after Asoka's death, it is one of the most popular religions in Asia and is counted as one of the five world religions.

control of his empire. So he based his teaching on Dharma.

What is Dharma?

Dharma is a complicated and vague Hindu idea which shows how societies should behave and be governed. Asoka said that it meant that people should be tolerant of one another's beliefs. They should not be violent to each other or to animals, unless no other course of action could be found.

The idea of Dharma extends into making life more comfortable and pleasant. Asoka built a network of roads to make travelling easier. There were rest houses and watering places along the way and Asoka planted trees to give shade. He ordered that wells should be dug to provide water for farming, and he set up mines and new industries to create more wealth.

The emperor trained officials to teach his new laws and beliefs. They were instructed to travel throughout the empire teaching people and putting the laws of Dharma into practice. These officials also travelled into neighbouring kingdoms outside the empire, persuading people to lead non-violent lives. This kept things peaceful on the borders of Asoka's empire for the whole of his reign.

Remarkable achievement

Sadly Asoka's empire did not survive his death. Some areas became separate states again, while invaders took over parts of central India. Buddhism also began to fade in India as an earlier religion, Hinduism, made a comeback. Yet the religion continued to flourish in other parts of Asia, largely as a result of Asoka's work.

The inscriptions on Asoka's pillars set out the laws of the land and the ways of the Buddhist faith. They were there for anyone to read who could.

Shih Huang Ti, Emperor of China

Shih Huang Ti was ruthless. A Qin from the west of China, he had driven his armies across mountains and plains to unify the warring kingdoms of China against the barbarian invaders from the north.
Nothing was allowed to stand in his way – scholars, nobles and local customs were crushed as he united China for the first time.

| 400 | BC/AD | 400 | 800 | 1200 | 1600 | 2000 |

221 BC Chang'an, China

The history of China can be traced back at least 4,000 years, but it was not until 221 BC that the whole country first came under one ruler. He was the ruthless First Emperor, Shih Huang Ti.

Before that time, China was divided into separate states ruled by powerful dynasties – there were certain periods when one family had more power and was acknowledged as the ruling dynasty by the surrounding states.

The Shang dynasty ruled over northern China from about 1750 to 1050 BC. The Shang were defeated by the Chou people from the valley of the River Wei. They became China's ruling dynasty for about 800 years.

Conquests by the Qin

At the end of the Chou period in 480 BC, the separate states were all at war, struggling for power. The constant battles

Shih Huang Ti (c.259–210 BC) came to the throne of the Qin dynasty at the age of 13. He believed in the absolute power of the ruler and was very harsh.

weakened the rival states and made way for the Qin, who came from western China and had one of the largest territories. The Qin began to conquer the other states, and by 221 BC the whole of China was united under one ruler.

Barbarian threat

The Qin ruler took the name Shih Huang Ti, which means 'First Emperor'. He had control of an area about the size of modern-day China, but his lands were being threatened by barbarian tribes from the north. The emperor did not want to see his new-found empire slip through his fingers. In order to keep invaders out and his own people in, Shih Huang Ti built the Great Wall of China by linking and strengthening fortifying walls which had already been built along the northern borders. The final wall stretched over 2,400 kilometres.

Important changes

Shih Huang Ti knew that some Chinese people resented the Qin because they had taken power by force. He was a determined and ruthless man, and he realized that he would have to make some changes if China was to remain united.

Powerful families were no longer allowed to control their own lands. They had to live in the capital city, Xianyang. A standard system of money, weights and measures was introduced. The emperor also broke up possible groups of trouble-makers by having them resettled in different areas.

Bonfire of knowledge

Chinese scholars (men of great learning) did not approve of many of these changes. To make them forget the past, the emperor ordered that most books should be destroyed. The famous 'Burning of the Books', particularly the works of Confucius (551–479 BC) and his followers, took place in 213 BC, and many influential scholars were put to death in the following year.

His dynasty ended four years after Shih Huang Ti's death in 210 BC, but his reign marks a turning point in Chinese history. His reforms paved the way for China's future greatness. His system of standard money and weights and measures encouraged trade which led to the development of the great trade routes through Central Asia, and extended China's influence in Asia.

Emperor Shih Huang Ti beside the Great Wall. Many thousands of workers died during its construction from disease, hunger, exhaustion and raids by barbarians. It is one of the great achievements of the world.

A section of the Great Wall of China.

FASCINATING FACTS

The Great Wall of China is the largest thing ever built – so big that it can be seen from the Moon. It has been changed and rebuilt since Shih Huang Ti's time. The wall that can be seen today was mainly built by the Ming dynasty (1368–1644).

Shih Huang Ti was very afraid of death. Soon after he became emperor, 700,000 workers began to build his tomb. When the emperor died, about 6,000 life-size soldiers made of pottery were buried in pits to guard the entrance to the tomb.

The Chinese could write and they invented paper. Over 2,500 years ago, they were interested in writing down the history of their people. These books were written by teams of scholars. Shih Huang Ti created one system of writing for the whole empire. Early histories were destroyed during the Burning of the Books. Only books on medicine, farming, religion and the history of the Qin dynasty were saved.

Chinese writing is based closely on the pictorial characters (symbols for portraying such things as fields, earth and pots) of the Shang dynasty, which lasted from about the eighteenth to the twelfth centuries BC.

Julius Caesar, Consul of Rome

'I came, I saw, I conquered,' Caesar said of his military successes in western Europe. At home in Rome, the same was also true. As dictator, he changed Rome's laws, and became very popular as he gave additional rights to many Roman colonies. He made it possible for the Roman Emperors who succeeded him to establish a lasting peace across the empire.

| 400 | BC/AD | 400 | 800 | 1200 | 1600 | 2000 |

44 BC Rome, Italy

The story of Rome and the great empire that grew from a village on the banks of the River Tiber is one of the most famous in history. The Romans were brilliant soldiers and engineers, and many of their achievements still remain today.

the Latin *res publica*, which means 'the thing belonging to everybody'. But this was not, in fact, true. The people were divided into two classes, the 'patricians', who were rich and powerful noblemen, and the 'plebeians' or working people. The patricians were the ruling class.

Dictator of Rome

When the Romans are mentioned, the name of one man springs to mind – Julius Caesar. He became dictator of Rome in 46 BC, and so marked the end of the Roman Republic, when there was no king or emperor and her leaders were elected by the people.

Rome was a republic for nearly 500 years. It was governed by two consuls and a senate of officials who were elected by the citizens each year. The word 'republic' comes from

Julius Caesar (100–44 BC) led the Roman to victory in many battles in Gaul (now France). After he and his army crossed the River Rubicon into Italy, the Roman Republic fell.

Greed and rebellion

The long wars against Carthage (an empire that dominated north Africa), which lasted on and off for over a hundred years from 264 BC, brought great victories for the Romans, but troubles at home.

Overseas conquests had made the patricians even more wealthy. They bought more land and used slaves to farm it. Successful army leaders were rewarded with gifts of land by the senate. But most people in Italy were poor farmers working a small plot of land. In

Many myths surrounded Caesar's death. It is said that Spurinna, the soothsayer, told Caesar to beware the Ides of March. Doctors and soothsayers warned Caesar not to go to the senate house on the day he was murdered. The night before, his wife, Calpurnia, had had nightmares and the ceremonial armour which Caesar kept in his house fell off the wall with a great crash.

Julius Caesar led the first Roman invasion of Britain in 55 BC. Britain later became a Roman province under the Emperor Claudius and many signs of Roman occupation remain today.

The writer Suetonius said that Caesar was 'a bit of a dandy. He always kept his hair carefully trimmed and used to comb his few hairs forward to cover his baldness.'

Roman legionaries with their 'eagle' or standard.

wartime, they had to fight in the Roman army and so could not farm their land.

The gifts of land to army leaders meant that the poor farmers were forced off their land and had to move into the towns and so many plebeians were out of work. The country was run by a few rich and powerful men, while other people starved.

The people rebel

The people rebelled against this situation and there was a long period of unrest. The senators tried to gain control of the people by sending an army commanded by two generals, Marius (157–86 BC) and Sulla (138–78 BC), to quell the rebels. But the generals themselves became rivals and began a civil war. Eventually, Sulla won control and became dictator for two

years. He retired in 79 BC and two of his officers, Crassus (c. 115–53 BC) and Pompey (106–48 BC), became consuls.

Meanwhile, Julius Caesar had been developing a career as a political leader, and was elected consul in 59 BC. In the same year, he formed the first 'triumvirate' – a governing trio of himself, Pompey and Crassus.

Brilliant soldier

Caesar soon proved himself to be a brilliant soldier. He conquered Gaul and brought many smaller states under Roman rule. These conquests made him more and more powerful and Pompey began to fear him. The senate tried to make Caesar give up command of his army, but he refused. So they gave Pompey the responsibility of defending Rome against Caesar.

Caesar and his army declared civil

war against Pompey by crossing the River Rubicon into Italy and marching on Rome, which fell to Caesar. Pompey fled to Greece. Caesar pursued him and defeated his army at Pharsalus in 48 BC. Pompey himself escaped to Egypt, where he was murdered.

Caesar becomes dictator of Rome

In 46 BC, after more conquests in Spain and Africa, Caesar was elected dictator of Rome. He ruled as a king and made many reforms. He limited the powers of the patricians, and made sure that plebeians and soldiers were resettled in Italy. Before then, only the people of Rome were counted as citizens, but Caesar extended this citizenship to include other peoples living in Italy.

He also introduced a revised calendar.

Many of the senators disliked the way Caesar ruled because they felt it was destroying the republic. But Caesar was not a harsh ruler. He did not have his opponents killed as his predecessors had done. This proved to be his downfall, because some of the senators began to plot against him. On 15 March 44 BC, Caesar was stabbed to death in the senate house.

End of the republic

The senators behind the plot were Cassius and Brutus. They did not succeed in their aims, however, for Caesar's death marked the end of the republic. There was a period of unrest, during which Cassius and Brutus were

The Roman empire at Caesar's death, 44 BC.

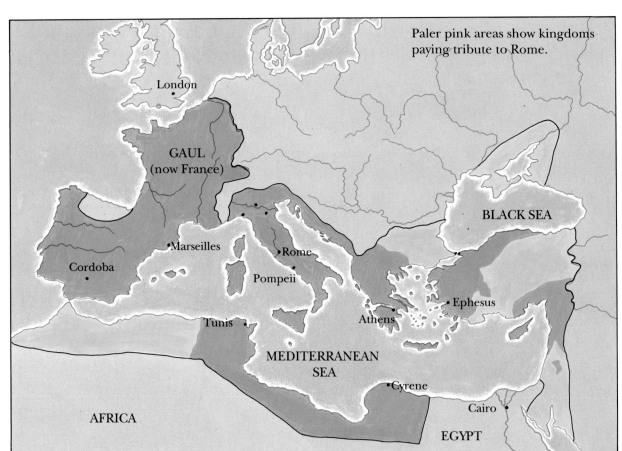

Paler pink areas show kingdoms paying tribute to Rome.

London

GAUL
(now France)

BLACK SEA

Marseilles

Cordoba

Rome

Pompeii

Ephesus

Tunis

Athens

MEDITERRANEAN
SEA

Cyrene

Cairo

AFRICA

EGYPT

killed by the next consul, Marcus
Antoninus (c. 83–30 BC). Then, in 30
BC, Caesar's great-nephew, Octavius
(63 BC–AD 14), became the first
emperor and took the name Augustus.
Caesar's reforms had made Rome and
her government more stable, and the
empire lasted for another 400 years.

*Julius Caesar was one of Rome's most
successful and influential rulers, but today he
is mainly remembered for his gruesome death on
the Ides of March. Led by Brutus and Cassius,
the senators stood round Caesar and stabbed
him twenty-three times. His last words, 'And
you too, my child?' were spoken to Brutus,
whose career he had helped.*

Constantine of Byzantium

By AD 300 the Roman Empire was dying – it was too big and had too many enemies. Constantine decided to cut his losses and build a new city from which to rule a smaller empire. He chose a site on the edge of the Bosporus for Constantinople. He also chose a new religion – Christianity. The empire he founded, Byzantium, lasted for over 1,200 years.

400	BC/AD		400	800	1200	1600	2000

325 AD Istanbul, Turkey

Christianity had spread after the death of Jesus Christ, but the Roman authorities would not accept the new religion. All the emperors were worshipped as gods. Because Christians only worshipped the one god, the Roman emperors realized this was a threat to their power. As a result, many Christians were killed or imprisoned for their beliefs. But then Emperor Constantine became a Christian and made Christianity the official religion of the Roman Empire in AD 324.

Rome in decline
The Roman empire had begun to decline by the time Constantine came to power. It had become too big for any one man to control, and barbarian tribes had begun to invade its borders. More soldiers were needed to defend the provinces – the outlying territories – of the empire against these invaders. Many of the generals saw a chance to become emperor. Civil war broke out, which led to the army becoming divided. Twenty Roman emperors were murdered between AD 211 and 284.

A rich and glittering city
Constantine became sole emperor in AD 312, having defeated his rivals. He did not see Christianity as a threat to his power. Instead, he realized that having one religion would unite the empire. So in AD 313 he ordered that Christians should be allowed to practise their religion in peace.

Constantine also decided that Rome was no longer a suitable capital of the empire. It had been overrun by barbarians, and too many people held to the old beliefs. So in AD 324 he began to build a new

A coin of Constantine the Great (c. AD 285–337). As emperor he made the Roman Empire Christian and founded the glittering city of Constantinople (now Istanbul).

capital. The site he chose for the new city was a port called Byzantium. Its position on the mouth of the Bosporus – a narrow strip of water linking the Black Sea and the Sea of Marmara in what is now Turkey – made it excellent for trading.

The city was modelled on Rome, but its buildings were even more lavish and splendid. Constantine planned to call the city New Rome, but it became known as Constantinople, meaning 'the city of Constantine'.

Byzantine civilization

Constantine was an excellent emperor and soldier. He had many battle victories and made his empire stable and strong again. His reign in his new city marked the start of what came to be known as the Byzantine civilization.

Before Constantine's time, there had been ceremonies of worship for the emperor. When Constantine converted to Christianity, these had to stop because no one could worship the emperor any more. However, the ceremonies were easily changed to Christian services. The emperor was now regarded as God's representative on earth. This gave him similar power to being regarded as a god himself.

Official religion

The layout of Roman temples, with their rectangular hall and aisles, formed the basis of church design for centuries to come. There were already churches in other parts of the empire, and their form of service was followed by the new Byzantine churches. Christianity became the official religion of the Roman Empire.

However, Christianity did not unite the empire in the way Constantine

The first Christian churches were built at this time.

FASCINATING FACTS

In AD 312, Constantine marched on Rome to meet his last rival, Maxentius, in battle. On the way he is said to have seen a shining cross in the sky and on it were written the words, 'By this, conquer'. He placed the cross (the sign of Christ) on his soldiers' shields and won a great victory against his rival, which left him sole ruler of the West.

❑

Despite his support for Christianity, Constantine did not become a Christian officially until AD 337. He was baptised on his deathbed. Stories of his baptism in Rome in AD 326 were made up later for political reasons.

❑

The Byzantines earned the money to build Constantinople by charging 10 per cent on all goods passing through the city. They bought grain from Egypt, silks from China, spices from the East Indies, gold and ivory from Africa, and furs and wood from Russia.

❑

Constantinople became so rich through trading that it was known as the Golden Horn. Byzantine gold coins became the trading currency for merchants from lands as far away as China.

hoped. Once it was the recognized faith, people began to argue about what true Christians should believe. Councils were organized to set down the exact rules of the Church. The first council called by Constantine in AD 325 produced the Nicene Creed, which is still used in Christian churches.

The empire falls

Barbarian invasions had continued in many Roman towns and this was to lead to the fall of the western half of the empire in AD 476. The eastern half, governed from Constantinople, then became known as the Byzantine Empire. From the time of Constantine, people regarded the Byzantine emperors as heads of the Christian

Constantine was a strong ruler whose decision to divide the empire into two – east and west – and set up a new capital at Constantinople made way for the Byzantine Empire after the fall of Rome. In 1930, the city was renamed Istanbul – it is now part of Turkey. Constantine's conversion to Christianity was a great step forward for the followers of Jesus Christ, for he allowed Christians to worship freely and without fear in his empire.

church, although Rome became the centre of Christianity. Constantine's decision to convert to Christianity and to make it the religion of his empire ensured that it became one of the major religions in the world. The decisions he made still affect the way many people in the world think today.

The Arch of Constantine in Rome was built to celebrate Constantine's victory over Maxentius in AD 312.

King John & the Magna Carta

The nobles of England were furious with their king. He had started wars and raised taxes without asking them first; he was treacherous and a liar. All the barons wanted was to stop the king acting like a tyrant, but the document that they made him sign gave a new and fundamental right to his subjects – that no-one should be imprisoned without a fair trial.

400   BC/AD   400   800   1200   1600   2000

1215 Runnimede, England

The Magna Carta, the document which John signed at Runnymede in 1215, is one of the most famous written statements in history. But what was the Magna Carta and why was it drawn up?

In 1199, when John came to the English throne, England had been at war with France for some years. The English royal family had rights over much of western France, from Normandy to south of Bordeaux. The previous king, Richard I, had been killed while fighting in south-western France.

Normandy is lost

John continued the struggle to protect his rights when he became king. In 1200, he married Isabella of Angoulême and so formed an alliance with an area to the west of the Limousin, a region of central France. But in 1204, the English lost Normandy to the French king, Philip II Augustus (1165–1223).

In 1206, John tried to capture Poitou, an area of central France which controlled several important roads. He did not succeed and, in 1214, he tried again. He managed to take the cities of Nantes and Angers and now wanted to fight the French king himself.

The barons object to taxes

These military campaigns were expensive, however, and had to be paid for out of taxes. The English barons (nobles) objected to being asked for more taxes for wars with France. They disliked John's unjust way of ruling the country – he used any method he could to raise money for his campaigns and made laws as it suited him, suddenly removing favours that he had granted to the barons.

The Great Seal of King John (1167–1216). John was the fourth and youngest son of Henry II and succeeded his brother, Richard the Lionheart in 1199.

They felt that he was too powerful, and that his policies abroad and at home were wrong. Proper laws of the land should be laid down, and people should have the right to speak out against injustice.

The barons take control of London

In 1215, the barons threatened to go to war with the king if he did not listen to their grievances. John made them promises which he did not keep, and the barons marched on London. By 17 May 1215, they controlled the whole city except the Tower of London.

More and more people joined the rebels, and the king was powerless to fight back. He realized that he would have to negotiate with the barons.

So a series of meetings took place in a meadow at Runnymede and a document called the 'Articles of the Barons' was drawn up. This was followed by the Magna Carta itself.

What the charter said

The Magna Carta contained laws which were designed to prevent the king from wielding too much power. The tax laws were reformed and there were laws about marriage, ownership of land, payment of debts and, most importantly, the way in which laws were enforced and justice was done.

Chapter 39 of the charter stated that, 'No freeman shall be arrested, or kept in prison, or disseised (have his lands taken away), or outlawed or banished, or in any way brought to ruin unless by the lawful judgement of his peers or by the law of the land'.

So the king had had to promise that everyone would be given a fair trial. The trials were to be conducted by justices (judges) who would visit

different parts of the country four times a year. There were also clauses protecting the rights of merchants and of cities, towns and ports. The barons were seeking to reform every aspect of life in England, and protect everyone from the king.

Problems with the charter

However, the Magna Carta was not foolproof. For one thing, it was not possible for the justices to get round the country four times a year. But the main problem was that there was no central court of justice to make sure that the clauses of the charter were put into practice.

The barons suggested that there should be a council of twenty-five barons to administer the rule of the charter. Four barons would be chosen from this council to hear complaints against the king and settle any disputes. This system was clearly open to a great deal of abuse. The barons could elect enemies of the king to the council and there was no one on it to represent the king's point of view.

Despite all this, the Magna Carta had a lasting influence. It was reissued with some changes in 1216, 1217 and 1225. However, it was to have an even greater influence in the seventeenth century, when lawyers on the side of Parliament used it as a statement of civil rights against the early Stuart kings of England. Its ideals were also taken to America where it helped to shape the Constitution of the United States.

Meetings between John and his barons led to the signing of the Magna Carta in 1215. The Magna Carta had an immense influence on English history because it stated that an English king could not govern as he liked.

The Catholic King & Queen

In January 1492, the Christian guns were pounding Granada in southern Spain. The last stronghold of the Islamic kings was about to surrender to Ferdinand and Isabella, who had united the rest of Spain. A great civilization and an era of history ended when Granada fell. Six months later Columbus sailed west from Cadiz and found the Americas, changing the world for ever.

| 400 | BC/AD | 400 | 800 | 1200 | 1600 | 2000 |

1490 Granada, Spain

Spain became a Roman province in about 145 BC. It was later converted to Christianity under Constantine the Great. About AD 415, it was taken over by the Visigoths, a Germanic people who ruled until 711, when Arab Moors from north Africa invaded southern Spain and defeated the last Visigoth king.

Moorish influence

The period of Moorish rule had a great influence on Spanish culture and architecture, but from AD 900 onwards, gradually the Christians won back their lands. By about 1240, Castile, León, Navarre and Aragon were separate Christian kingdoms. Only Granada, in the south of Spain, was still under Moorish rule.

The various Christian kingdoms went on fighting each other for power for more than 200

Ferdinand II of Aragon (1452–1516), married Isabella of Castile (1451–1504) in 1469. She inherited Castile in 1474. When he inherited Aragon in 1479, they united Spain.

years. The strongest of these kingdoms were Castile and Aragon. Castile formed an alliance with León and its power spread southwards towards Granada. By the beginning of the fifteenth century, most of central and northern Spain was under the control of Castile. Aragon, in eastern Spain, had been a strong trading kingdom, but its trade had declined by the fifteenth century. The Black Death, which swept through Europe from the East in the fourteenth century, had also depleted the population. Then, in 1469, Ferdinand the Catholic, the heir to the throne of Aragon, married Isabella of Castile. When he

The Castilians used up-to-date methods of warfare. The huge army gathered outside Granada and trapped the Muslim people within. It forced the city to negotiate with Ferdinand and finally to surrender to the Spaniards.

The Alhambra palace in Granada is a fine example of Moorish architecture.

FASCINATING FACTS

The Arabic name for Gibraltar is Jabal Tariq which means 'Tariq's Mountain'. It was named after the Moorish leader Tariq ibn Ziyad who invaded southern Spain and defeated the Visigoths.

The Moors brought the culture of Islam into Spain. They called their Spanish territory al-Andalus. It was a centre of learning and the arts. The Moorish architecture, with its domes and arched windows, can still be seen in Spain today.

Ferdinand and Isabella were strong rulers and were determined to keep their rebellious nobles under control. They stopped giving them government posts and instead used paid civil servants to help in the government of the country.

Ferdinand and Isabella gave Christopher Columbus the financial backing he needed for his voyage of exploration in 1492. Columbus was trying to find a western route to the Spice Islands (now known as the Moluccas). Instead, he found the islands of the West Indies, and so began the Spanish exploration and conquest of Central and South America.

became king in 1479, the two kingdoms were united.

So the Catholic king and queen ruled over most of Christian Spain. Now they turned their eyes to the Moorish kingdom of Granada. The Castilians had a strong army and in 1482 they began a series of attacks on different parts of the kingdom. One by one, the Moorish towns began to fall.

The fall of Granada

The Moorish rulers were not always loyal to one another and Ferdinand took advantage of this. He negotiated with Boabdil, one of the sons of the king of Granada, who agreed to go to war against his father.

The city of Málaga fell in 1487, which gave Ferdinand control of the western part of the Moorish lands. Now only the city of Granada remained under Moorish rule. But then Boabdil changed his mind and decided to fight for Granada. Enraged, Ferdinand and his army massed outside the city. On 2 January 1492, the city surrendered to the Spaniards.

Christian Spain

The Moors were allowed to stay in their region. They could practise their Muslim religion and live by their own laws and customs. This worked for a time, but some Spaniards feared that the Moors might rebel against Spanish rule. The Muslims were forced to convert to Christianity and this led to revolts. Eventually, most of the Moors were expelled to north Africa.

Now Spain was a completely Christian country again. This marked a new beginning. The stage was set for Spain's great period of exploration and the conquest of other lands.

Cortés & the Aztec Empire

Cortés staggered down the the steps of the pyramid, sick to the pit of his stomach. He had just watched the sacrifice to the sun, when living hearts were ripped from men's chests. Disgust for the savagery of the Aztecs was added to his desire for their gold. His mind was made up at last – the Aztec Empire must be destroyed.

| 400 | BC/AD | 400 | 800 | 1200 | 1600 | 2000 |

1521 Mexico City, Mexico

The tales Columbus and his sailors brought back to Spain about the new lands across the Atlantic Ocean fired the imaginations of other Spanish explorers. There was great wealth to be found in the newly discovered lands. The Catholic Church in Spain was also keen to convert other peoples to Christianity. During the early sixteenth century, expeditions set out to explore this 'New World'. The Spanish conquered vast areas of land and changed the local way of life forever.

Rise of the Aztecs
The first great Spanish conquest was the defeat of the mighty Aztec Empire by Hernan Cortés in 1519. The Aztecs had built a huge city, Tenochtitlan (*say it:* Ten-ock-tit-lan), on the site of what is now Mexico City. From this city they governed an empire which covered a

Hernan Cortés (1485–1547), the Spanish conquistador who defeated the Aztecs with a few hundred men. Some say that he was a great leader, others that he was greedy for gold.

large part of modern Central America.

The early Aztecs were a wandering tribe of hunters and farmers who probably arrived in Mexico in the thirteenth century. After travelling from place to place for many years, they finally reached Lake Texcoco in about 1325. This swampy lake with a large island in the middle was to be site of their city, Tenochtitlan. In less than 200 years it had become one of the largest cities in the world.

The city grows
As the city grew, the Aztecs drained the swamps to make more land for building and farming. The city was criss-crossed by canals and people travelled by boat. Three stone causeways (raised paths) linked the city to the mainland.

By the time the Spaniards arrived, about

200,000 people lived in Tenochtitlan. The empire had become large and powerful. It was ruled by a succession of kings, the last of whom was Montezuma II.

The Aztecs conquered the neighbouring tribes in the Valley of Mexico and set up trading links with peoples outside the empire. They were skilled craftworkers – their merchants travelled throughout the empire and

beyond, selling goods and buying the raw materials the craftworkers needed.

'Winged Towers'

The Aztecs had no idea that there were any lands beyond the seas. In 1519, messengers brought Montezuma news of 'winged towers' (ships) on the sea and white men with beards who had landed on the east coast and were coming to Tenochtitlan. The Aztecs

were very afraid. The Spaniards later claimed that they remembered an old legend about Quetzalcoatl (*say it:* Ket-zul-co-atul), the Plumed Serpent God. Quetzalcoatl was supposed to have disappeared across the sea, saying that he would return to claim his kingdom. Montezuma may have thought the visitors from across the sea were gods.

As he did not want the visitors to come to Tenochtitlan, Montezuma

The Aztecs watched in bewilderment as the lines of Spanish soldiers approached Tenochtitlan. They had never seen horses or guns before. The Spaniards were equally amazed by their first sight of Tenochtitlan. The sheer size of the city astonished them. Many of the great buildings were still almost new and their stonework gleamed in the sunshine. The Spanish soldier Bernal Diaz described the city as full of 'gleaming white towers and castles: a marvellous sight'.

sent priests and warriors to the coast with lavish gifts for them and warnings to stay away. But Cortés wanted to get to the city where all these precious gifts came from, so he and his army started off on the long overland journey to Tenochtitlan.

The journey took several months and there was fierce fighting. But the Spaniards always won and some of the defeated peoples even joined the Spanish army.

Two cultures collide

Cortés arrived at Tenochtitlan on 8 November 1519. The meeting of the two very different civilizations must have been a shock to both of them. The Spaniards, who had ruthless methods of warfare, wanted to take over new lands and gain more wealth.

The Aztecs were brave fighters, but they had different methods of warfare. When they fought wars, they aimed to take live prisoners to sacrifice to their many gods. This was to be their downfall. Although the Spaniards were outnumbered, they planned their attacks carefully to make the best use of men and weapons. While the Aztecs attacked in force and tried to take prisoners, the Spaniards simply killed as many as they could.

Montezuma and Cortés came to an agreement, and the Spaniards settled down as guests in the city. But this situation did not last for long. When Cortés was called away from the city, he left his deputy, Alvarado, in charge. Trouble broke out between Alvarado and the Aztecs, and the Aztecs imprisoned the Spaniards in the palace.

When Cortés returned, he persuaded Montezuma to release Cortés' men and restrain his people. This made the Aztecs very angry; they turned against Montezuma and stoned him to death.

The final battle

Now there was no hope of a peace in the Aztec city. Cortés took his army away so that he could decide what to do next. Some of his men had been killed, but he managed to get more support from other cities who wanted an end to Aztec control.

Cortés came back and blockaded the

Aztec warriors fought to take prisoners, not to kill their enemies. This was because the temples (right) needed a constant supply of human hearts to offer to the gods.

city. They cut off the water supply and made an all-out attack. In April 1521, Tenochtitlan fell to the Spaniards.

Ten years after the conquest, the whole of Mexico was under Spanish rule with Cortés as governor. He ordered Tenochtitlan to be destroyed and a new city to be built on the site. Catholic churches replaced the Aztec temples. The new city of Mexico became the capital of New Spain.

The people of the Aztec empire had lived so long under powerful rulers that at first they did not resent the Spaniards, who treated them well. The Catholic priests who arrived to convert them to Christianity learned the Aztec language, Nahuatl (*say it*: Na-hoo-atul), and taught them about religion, reading and writing.

The church also sent word that no people must be ill-treated or used as slaves, but little notice was taken of this. Cortés was not a cruel man, but he was determined to find wealth, so he took everything he could from the Aztecs. Huge quantities of gold and treasures were sent back to Spain, which then paid for wars in Europe.

New conquests
Other Spanish conquests in South America followed. Of these, the defeat of the Incas of Peru by Francisco Pizarro (c. 1478–1541) in 1533 was particularly important because it provided the Spaniards with another empire and a source of great wealth.

Spanish settlers travelled to the new lands and much of Central and South America became Spanish speaking, as it is today. In time, the Spanish Catholic civilization blended with the native populations, and a unique group of cultures developed.

Ivan IV unites Russia

Ivan, first Tsar of Russia, sat on his throne and worried. He knew that his nobles, the boyars, were plotting against him. What he needed was an enemy who would unite all the people of Russia behind him. The obvious target was the Tatar stronghold of Kazan – source of hundreds of raids on Russia – but the risks of attacking such a strong fortress were immense....

400	BC/AD	400	800	1200		1600	2000

1547 Moscow, Russia

After many centuries of unrest, Russia was finally united under one ruler (or tsar) in 1547. The tsar was Ivan IV and his reign began a line of tsars which lasted until the Russian Revolution in 1917. He united Russia, which had previously been divided into separate states. Yet Ivan IV had a reputation for such cruelty that he earned the name Ivan the Terrible. So who was this man and what led up to his reign of terror?

Take-over by the Tatars
Russia became a Christian civilization in AD 988, when Grand Prince Vladimir of Kiev converted to the religion.

From 1237 to 1240, the Tatars, who were savage horsemen from the Mongolian empire, swept in and conquered most of Russia, killing many people and burning whole towns to the ground. Many years of

brutality followed until the Tatars were finally weakened by rivalries between their own rulers. In Russia, Ivan III (1440–1505), known as the Great who was Grand Prince of Muscovy from 1462 to 1505, took advantage of this. He regained lands held by the Tatars and managed to break free from Tatar rule.

Ivan the Terrible (1530–84) was Grand Prince of Muscovy from the age of three and crowned tsar in 1547. From 1560, his reign was spoiled by acts of dreadful cruelty.

Elena is made regent
Ivan IV was born in 1530. His father, Vasily, was Ivan the Great's grandson. Vasily died when the boy was only three years old. His mother, Elena, was made regent, which meant that she took charge of running the country while Ivan was still too young to run the country himself.

A power struggle began between the boyars – powerful nobles at the Russian court – and Elena. Then, in 1538, Elena suddenly died. It seemed certain that she had been poisoned. The young Ivan was now completely at the mercy of the ruthless boyars, who were only interested in seizing power for themselves. The atmosphere at court was one of plotting, scheming and cruelty. People were tortured or murdered on a whim.

Fear of being murdered

Against this background, Ivan began to take cruelty as a normal way of life. He hated the boyars, but he was also very afraid of them. He lived in fear of being murdered and became suspicious of everyone around him. This period in his life helped to form the character that later earned him the name 'the Terrible'.

But during the early years of his reign, Ivan was a great ruler. As he grew up, he began to set his sights on lands outside the borders of Muscovy. He knew that the state needed a strong ruler, and he was determined to reduce the powers of the boyars. At his coronation in 1547, he was crowned as the tsar. This title (derived from the Latin word, *Caesar*) put the ruler far above other princes and the boyars.

The conquest of Kazan

Ivan's first problem as tsar was to quell the Tatars who still held the land to the east and frequently crossed the borders into Russian territory. He conquered the Tatar strongholds of Kazan, in 1552, and Astrakhan in 1554.

The conquest of Kazan is one of the most famous victories in Russian history. The Russians besieged the fortress city and made several attempts to storm it. They attacked with guns and cannons, and their explosives ripped holes in the walls, but the

FASCINATING FACTS

The capital of Muscovy was Moscow, which had grown from a small trading town to a large city. Ivan the Great established the Kremlin, or citadel, as the centre of administration and religion for the Russian state.

—— ❏ ——

Ivan the Great made many people into serfs, growing the grain that was needed to feed the population. They were not allowed to leave their land or their master.
Some of the serfs rebelled and fled to the south where they formed bands of rebels known as Cossacks. The threat of rebellion from the Cossacks was a danger to Moscow for centuries.

—— ❏ ——

Ivan the Terrible was not always successful in his conquests. He wanted an outlet into the Baltic Sea which he felt would help Russian trade with the West. But his conquest of Livonia, on the Baltic coast, was defeated by the Lithuanians, Poles and Swedes.

—— ❏ ——

During the final attack on Kazan, Ivan was at prayer and refused to join his army. When he finally agreed to go to the city, the Russian flag was already flying over the ruins.

A group of boyars wearing their traditional dress.

Tatars fought back relentlessly. Finally, the Russians scaled the walls with ladders. The trapped Tatars threw rocks and boiling water on to their attackers, and many Russians were killed. But this did not stop the others. They surged over the walls and engaged in fierce hand-to-hand fighting until the Tatars surrendered.

The conquest of Kazan was the one event which drew the states of Russia together. It was also the first time that non-Russian peoples had become Russian subjects.

The terror begins

For the first thirteen years of his reign, Ivan governed Russia wisely and was deemed an excellent ruler. But the death of his beloved wife, Anastasia, in 1560, changed all that. Ivan nearly went mad. He would fly into rages and have people tortured or put to death.

When he was no longer content with punishing individuals, he killed whole towns of people. In one rage, in 1581, Ivan struck his eldest son with such a fearsome blow that he killed him.

The head of the Russian Orthodox church, the Metropolitan, spoke out against the tsar's cruelties, so Ivan had him strangled. Now he had earned his name, 'Ivan the Terrible', and people lived in fear of him. But not before he had united Russia, and paved the way for the expansion of its empire.

Ivan's troops attacking Kazan in 1552. Many Russians died scaling the walls, but once the attackers were inside, there was fierce hand-to-hand fighting. Eventually the Tartars surrendered. The taking of Kazan happened during the early years of Ivan's reign when he ruled wisely and justly – the death of his wife in 1560 was followed by a reign of terror.

The Manchu Empire in China

The messenger galloped into the Manchu camp. 'Where is Prince Dorgon?'
he cried, 'The Ming Emperor has killed himself.' In 1644,
China was being torn apart by rebel armies. The only force strong enough
to take control was the invading army from Manchuria. Prince Dorgon
seized his opportunity and captured an empire for his 7-year-old nephew.

| 400 | BC/AD | 400 | 800 | 1200 | 1600 | 2000 |

1643 Beijing, China

The Ming dynasty ruled in China for nearly 300 years, during which time the arts flourished, particularly the making of fine china. However, the dynasty began to crumble in the early seventeenth century and, in 1644, China was conquered by foreign invaders, the Manchus. The Manchus were a nomadic people from Manchuria, a region on China's north-eastern borders. They founded the Qing dynasty, which ruled the Chinese empire until 1911.

Starving people
The successful Ming dynasty was badly affected by many events during the early seventeenth century. Trade had weakened and crops failed because of long periods of drought and flooding. Famines and outbreaks of the disease smallpox caused millions of deaths. The price of food rose, and many of the ordinary people starved.

Prince Dorgon (1612–50) ruled China for the Qing child emperor from 1644 until his death. He helped to found the Qing dynasty which ruled China until 1911.

The emperor had a massive and expensive palace in his capital Peking (now Beijing). There were nearly 20,000 eunuchs (men operated upon so that they could not have children) at court. They guarded the emperor's many wives, and also collected rents and taxes, supervised the guards and formed a secret police force. The eunuchs became very powerful and often siphoned off some of the money they collected for their own use. More taxes were raised to try to pay for the luxury at court, and starving people began to rebel against Emperor Chongzhen.

The Manchus attack
The way was open for the Manchus. They had already made some small attacks along the Chinese frontiers. Some Chinese nobles, seeing that the Ming Empire

was collapsing and seeking power for themselves, joined the side of the Manchus. They told the Manchus about rebellions brewing against the emperor, and advised them how and when to attack the cities.

The Manchu emperor, Huing Taiji, died in 1643 and his 6-year-old son succeeded him. The Manchu empire was ruled by Huing Taiji's half brother, Dorgon, and a famous general, called Jirgalang. Dorgon quickly proved himself to be a brilliant general and a stronger ruler than Jirgalang.

In 1644, the Manchus learned that the Ming emperor had killed himself and that the Chinese rebels were looting and pillaging their cities. The Ming prince appealed to Dorgon for help. In return for fighting the rebels the Manchus would receive territory and wealth from China.

Dorgon becomes ruler

Dorgon saw this as his chance to become ruler of China. First, he declared that the Manchu armies should fight against the rebels, but that there should be no needless killing or violence. In this way the Manchus would appear to be a better alternative to the rebels.

After a particularly bloody massacre by the Chinese rebel armies, in which many people were killed and buildings burned, Dorgon and his army moved in to take the Forbidden City, the home of the royal palace in Peking.

The people of the city were told by the Manchus that the Ming prince had agreed to Dorgon being their prince-regent, which meant that Dorgon was now their new ruler. The people were shocked and frightened as Dorgon entered the royal palace.

FASCINATING FACTS

Some of the Manchu ways were not welcome to the Chinese. For centuries, Chinese men had worn their hair long and in elaborate hairstyles under a cap. Now they were ordered to shave their foreheads and wear their hair in a pigtail. This was the tribal hairstyle of the Manchu people.

In 1645, Dorgon became "imperial uncle prince-regent." Orders were issued about how all other princes and nobles must bow to him. But Dorgon was supreme and bowed to no one.

The royal palace was known as the Forbidden City because commoners were not allowed to enter.

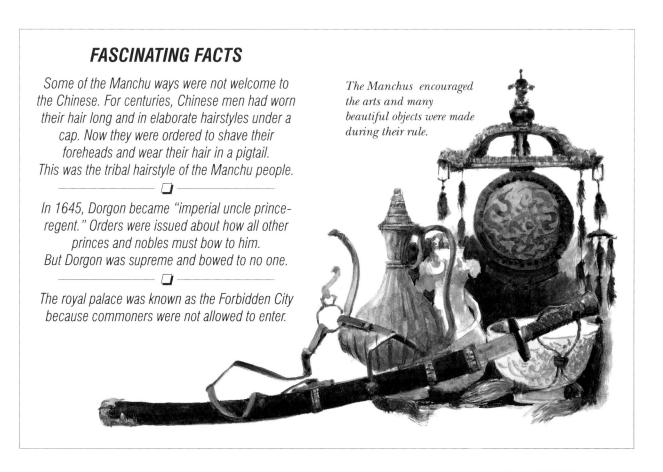

The Manchus encouraged the arts and many beautiful objects were made during their rule.

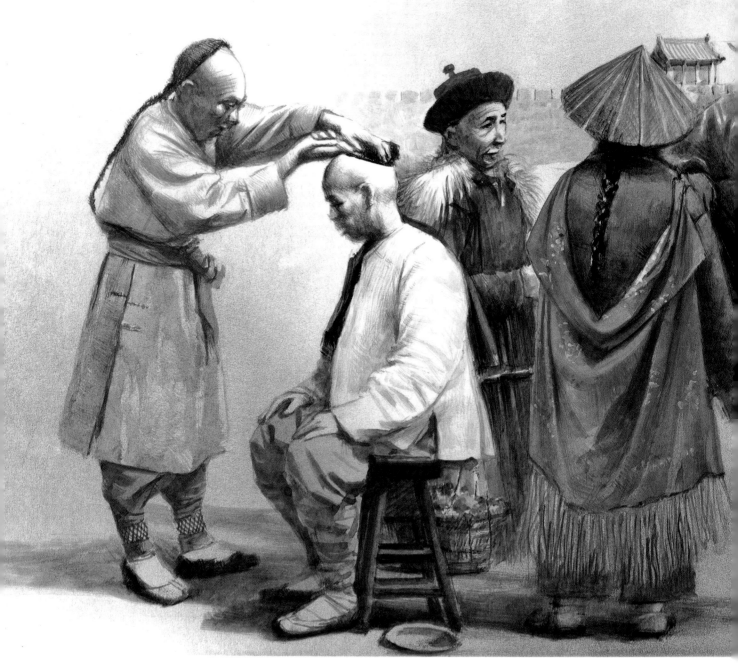

A cultural revolution

At first, many Chinese people were relieved to be in a stable situation again. And Dorgon made it plain that former Ming officials would be welcome in his new government. Even so, it took some years for the Manchus to become accepted and for them to establish their Qing dynasty.

There were many differences to overcome and some of the Qing changes were unpopular. The Manchu capital was moved to Peking, thus combining the two empires, and the young emperor, Shunzhi, was taken there. At a special ceremony proclaiming him emperor of China, the little boy was given a speech to recite in which he made Dorgon the 'uncle prince-regent', giving him power over General Jirgalang.

During Ming times, princes had governed separate provinces of the empire. Now Dorgon introduced a

central government, with everyone reporting directly to the throne. The rituals of the Confucian religion were adopted at the Qing court.

A period of prosperity followed the Qing take-over. The Manchu emperors were admirers of Chinese culture, and the arts were encouraged. And so the Qing managed to weld together two different cultures and hold on to their control over China until they were overthrown in a revolution in 1911.

A change of male hairstyle introduced by a Manchu ruling in 1645 was humiliating to the Chinese, who thought it a barbarian style. Some were beheaded rather than shave their foreheads. The ruling provoked an uprising among the peasants, who thought that cutting off their hair took away their manhood. This rebellion was known as the Jiangnan Resistance Movement. However, the Manchu pigtail was soon the accepted hairstyle for Chinese men. Ming dress – a flowing robe with a wide sash – was also abandoned at court.

The Defenestration of Prague

*Ferdinand II of Bohemia leapt to his feet in outrage. 'They did what?'
he shouted, 'They dared to throw my officials out of a window?'
It was the final confrontation between a Catholic king and his Protestant
nobles. Ferdinand sent an army to avenge the insult, other rulers joined in
on both sides, and a war that would last thirty years, was under way....*

| 400 | BC/AD | 400 | 800 | 1200 | 1600 | 2000 |

1618 Prague, Czech Republic

In 1617, Ferdinand of Habsburg (1578–1637) came to the throne of Bohemia, a central European state now part of the Czech Republic. Ferdinand II was a Roman Catholic and became Holy Roman Emperor two years later. He tried to enforce his religious views on the people of Bohemia, but this made him extremely unpopular as many Bohemians were Protestants – Christians who were separated from the Roman Catholic Church.

Protests ignored

The unrest came to a head in the capital city of Prague, when the Catholic Archbishop ordered that two Protestant churches should be closed down.
The Protestants' protests were ignored by the emperor, and so a group of powerful Protestant noblemen met with three of the

emperor's officials at Hradcany Castle in Prague. Again their protests failed, so the noblemen threw the officials out of the upper-floor windows. Luckily, the officials landed on a rubbish heap, so they lived to tell the tale!
The people decided to take the law into their own hands, and riots broke out in Prague. They also removed Ferdinand from the throne, and in 1619, offered it to Frederick V, the Protestant Elector of the Palatinate (in the Rhineland of Germany).
Ferdinand retaliated by gaining the support of Maximilian, Duke of Bavaria. This was the beginning of the Thirty

Frederick V (1596–1632) married Elizabeth Stuart, daughter of James I of England. They were known as the 'Winter King and Queen', because they only reigned for six months.

The emperor could not ignore the insult when his officials were thrown out of the castle windows. The dispute brought years of political and religious unrest to a head and led to the Thirty Years War in Europe.

During the Thirty Years War, the local population was in constant danger from raids from both sides. Thousands of civilians were killed, and millions lost possessions to the various armies based in central Europe during this time.

FASCINATING FACTS

In 1555, the Peace of Augsburg stated that the religion of a German ruler should determine the religion of the people. There was peace until Ferdinand came to the throne of Bohemia.

❑

The Thirty Years War was not nonstop fighting, because armies are expensive to keep going. The official fighting was conducted mostly in summer, with soldiers kept to a minimum.

Years War in Europe. The emperor's forces defeated the Bohemians in 1620, but the war escalated as the Netherlands and Denmark became involved on the Protestant side and Spain on the Catholic side. The Danes were defeated by the imperial forces and withdrew from the war in 1629 but, in 1630, Sweden stepped in on the Protestant side. They had a string of victories against the emperor, but the fighting continued.

Then in 1635, France (a Catholic country) entered the conflict. The French king, Louis XIII (1601–43), did not want the Holy Roman Emperor to gain more power in central Europe, so France supported the Protestants.

The last years of the war became a political struggle between France and the Holy Roman Empire. The war had caused so much death and devastation throughout Europe that in the 1640s the European states began to negotiate for a peace settlement. Although France and Spain continued their conflict until 1659, most countries reached an agreement, the Peace of Westphalia, in 1648.

Change in the balance of power

The main result of the peace treaty was to switch power in Europe from the emperor or Spanish ruler to the king of France. Separate states in Germany, the Netherlands and Switzerland, which had come under the Holy Roman Empire's rule, were recognized as being independent. The Lutherans and Calvinists – two Protestant groups – gained equal rights with the Roman Catholics. So the uprising in Prague had far-reaching effects and changed the political outlook of Europe.

The Fall of the Bastille

In 1789, the National Assembly of France and King Louis XVI were at loggerheads. The Assembly wanted to reform the king's inefficient and corrupt government and empower the people. The citizens of Paris believed that the king was about to strike back, so they alarmed themselves and destroyed a symbol of his tyranny – the dreaded prison of the Bastille.

400	BC/AD	400	800	1200	1600		2000

1789 Paris, France

By the late eighteenth century, tensions had built up to exploding point in France. The king, Louis XVI, did not rule his country properly, and lived for the pleasures of hunting. His wife, Marie Antoinette, was vain and spent her money wastefully. Yet Louis and his ministers had absolute power over the people. The people wanted freedom from the rule of kings and queens, and they were prepared to fight for it. This led to the French Revolution and the beginning of the republic of France.

Divided people

At this time, France was a powerful country which dominated Europe. But its people were divided into four groups, and there was great bitterness between them. First, there were the aristocrats who owned about one-fifth of the land in France and

Louis XVI (1754–93), king of France married Marie Antoinette of Austria (1755–93) in 1770. She supported the French aristocrats when they opposed tax reforms.

did not have to pay taxes. Their privileges made them unpopular, but they in turn resented the power the king's ministers had over the country.

The second group was the clergy. Most clergymen were not wealthy, but the Catholic Church also held large areas of land, and some high-ranking churchmen were very rich. The clergy had special privileges as well, which made them unpopular with everyone else.

Next came the 'bourgeoisie', or middle class, who were becoming as rich as the nobles, but were not entitled to the same privileges.

At the bottom of society were the peasants. Some peasants owned land, but only enough to feed themselves. Many of them had to do other work to survive. The peasants had to pay

money to their local lord as well as hefty taxes to the state.

Despite the heavy taxation, France had financial problems and, by the late 1780s, the government had no more money to pay its debts. King Louis appointed new finance ministers who proposed new taxes, which would hit the rich landowners hardest.

The scheme was very unpopular with the aristocrats, and in 1789, Louis was forced to call together a committee called the Estates General to vote on the taxes. This committee was made up of representatives from the nobility, the clergy and the middle class (also known as the 'Third Estate').

Power of the king condemned

Louis expected the committee to vote for the taxes, but the representatives saw a chance to do much more. The meetings were dominated by the Third Estate who thought of themselves as the true voice of the people.

The Estates General condemned the power of the king and adopted a charter, 'The Declaration of the Rights of Man', which had been drawn up by middle-class revolutionaries. This charter said that all men are born free and equal in rights and set out the basic rights of the citizen, such as freedom of speech and the right to own property. They also proposed church and government reforms.

On 17 June 1789, the Estates General voted to change its name to

There were only seven prisoners in the Bastille when it was stormed by a crowd of Parisian citizens on 14 July 1789. But the people of Paris saw the fortress as a symbol of the power the king held over the people. The Bastille was totally demolished after the attack.

The Estates General had not met since 1614. Then, it had consisted of equal numbers from each group – nobility, church and middle classes. This meant that the nobility and church could always out-vote the middle classes.
In 1789, the middle classes were given double the number of representatives, which made them the largest group on the committee.

❏

When Marie Antoinette was told that the people of Paris were starving because there was no bread, she made the famous sharp reply, 'If they have no bread, let them eat cake'. Her arrogant attitude contributed to the unpopularity of the monarchy. She was guillotined in September 1793.

❏

Georges Danton and Maximilien Robespierre were leaders of the extremist Jacobin party. The Jacobins fought for the republic, had the king executed and overthrew the more moderate Girondins. 'The king must die,' Robespierre said in one of his speeches, 'so that the state may live.'

❏

Robespierre was inspired by the French philosopher, Jean-Jacques Rousseau, who began his Social Contract with the famous sentence, 'Man is born free, but everywhere he is in chains'. Rousseau believed that people should be free to lead simple lives where everyone was equal. The Declaration of the Rights of Man reflects these ideas of freedom and equality.

Revolutionaries storm the Bastille.

the National Assembly. Louis was furious at all this and forbade the Assembly to meet again. The members defied him and swore that they would not go home until their proposed new laws had been passed.

Storming the Bastille

Meanwhile, rebellion was brewing on the streets of Paris. The harvest of 1788 had been bad, and there was a threat of famine. The price of bread had risen and the streets were crowded with starving people who expected the Assembly to help them. But they became tired of the long debates that seemed to lead nowhere. On 14 July 1789, the citizens took all the guns and cannons they could lay their hands on and attacked the Bastille.

The Bastille was a large stone fortress which was used as a prison. When the mob massed outside its walls, the governor of the prison tried to negotiate with them. But the people were impatient, and some of them managed to get into the fortress. Two hours of fighting followed during which the Bastille was sacked and the governor was killed. His head was put on to a pike and carried through the streets by the triumphant mob.

Louis is forced to give in

The fall of the Bastille was the turning point in the French Revolution. The people saw that they could use violence to get what they wanted. In the countryside outside Paris, there was rioting and the homes of some aristocrats were burned. The National Assembly proposed reforms that would limit the power of the king and abolish the aristocracy's privileges. At first the king refused to accept these measures.

(above) The philosopher, Jean-Jacques Rousseau (1712–78), whose ideas of freedom and equality inspired the Declaration of the Rights of Man and Robespierre.

(right) Maximilien Robespierre was known as the 'Sea-green Incorruptible' because he refused all bribes. After his execution, thousands of people who had been arrested during the Reign of Terror were released from prison.

for beheading people – and executed. Eight months later, his queen, Marie Antoinette, was tried and executed.

France declared herself a republic – the first in Europe since ancient Rome – but there was more trouble to follow. With the king dead, rival parties within the Assembly came forward. The new minister of justice, Georges Danton (1759–94), put forward a constitution – a set of rules and laws by which a country is governed – for the republic. But there were more rebellions against the revolution, and so the Reign of Terror began.

The Reign of Terror

Maximilien Marie Isidore Robespierre (1758–94) was a lawyer and a revolutionary leader whose moving speeches won wild support from the people. Robespierre condemned to death anyone who was opposed to the revolution, and about 1,500 aristocrats and anti-revolutionaries were sent to the guillotine. But the people of Paris turned against Robespierre and other leaders of this Reign of Terror. They were themselves sent to the guillotine in 1794.

The ideals of the French Revolution lived on when the new republic was formed. The *Declaration of the Rights of Man* had beguwn by stating that 'all men are born free and equal in rights'. It was an inspiration to ordinary people who had lived under the absolute rule of cruel monarchs, and now it helped to shape a new society run for the benefit of all.

Then, three months after the storming of the Bastille, the women of Paris marched on the palace at Versailles, and the king was forced to give in.

The end of the monarchy

The king tried to get his influential friends to raise armies against the revolution and restore his power, but he had lost his following and many nobles fled from France. New and more extreme leaders of the revolution came to power.

In 1792, a second revolution began, and the king was arrested and imprisoned. In January 1793, he was taken to the guillotine – an instrument

Bolívar in South America

When Simón Bolívar visited Europe in 1804, he saw for himself how the kingdoms of Europe were falling before Napoleon. Returning to South America, he raised the standard of freedom and led that enormous continent in its struggle to throw off its chains and gain independence from Spanish rule.

| 400 | BC/AD | 400 | 800 | 1200 | 1600 | 2000 |

1825 South America

After the Spanish and Portuguese conquests in South America, a steady flow of settlers left Europe for Latin America. The Europeans knew that there was money to be made in these newly conquered lands. There were riches, such as gold and silver, to be brought back to Europe, and there were vast tracts of land to farm. European settlers set up plantations in South America, where they grew coffee, cotton or sugar. Between 1500 and 1800, colonies of Europeans were established all over South America.

By 1800, the South American population consisted of native South Americans, people of European descent who had been born in South America, and *mestizos* or people of mixed race. Most of South America was ruled from Spain, and the people had very little

Simón Bolívar (1783–1830) admired thinkers like the French philosopher, Jean-Jacques Rousseau, who inspired him to free his people from Spanish rule.

freedom. The South American colonies were only allowed to trade with Spain and Portugal, which restricted the amount of money they could earn from exporting the goods they produced.

Fight for independence

These problems united the people of South America. They did not think of themselves as separate colonies, but as a nation who would have to fight for independence. They saw what could be achieved by fighting back when a former slave, Toussaint L'Ouverture (1746–1803), led a successful struggle against the French in Haiti, on the Caribbean island of Hispaniola.

Spain and Portugal were beginning to lose their power in Europe. In 1807, the French general and emperor, Napoleon Bonaparte

(1762–1821), invaded and occupied Portugal. In 1808, he deposed the king of Spain, Ferdinand VII, and put his brother, Joseph Bonaparte, on the throne. Now it was time for the people of South America to start their fight.

The people of Brazil did not have to fight for their independence. Brazil was a Portuguese colony. The king of Portugal, John VI, lived there during Napoleon's occupation of Portugal. When John returned to Portugal in 1821, he left his son Pedro to rule the colony. Pedro declared Brazil independent in 1822, and this was recognized by John in 1825, when his son became Pedro I, Emperor of Brazil.

The fight for freedom

The story was different in the Spanish colonies, in the areas that are known as Ecuador, Colombia, Bolivia, Panama, and Venezuela. Spain would not give up her empire without a struggle, and fighting broke out. Some great military leaders now emerged – one of the most important was Simón Bolívar.

Bolívar was born in Caracas, now in Venezuela, in 1793. As a young man, he visited Europe where he was influenced by philosophers, such as Rousseau, who talked of freedom and equality. Bolívar vowed then to free his country from Spanish rule.

Bolívar returned to South America in 1810 to find that rebellions had broken out in the struggle for freedom. Bolívar joined the rebels and soon became their leader. The rebels took Caracas in that year and declared independence from Spain in 1811. However, Bolívar was forced to leave the country and the new-found independence was lost. Bolívar returned in 1813 and made Caracas

San Martin and the memorial to his liberation of Chile.

FASCINATING FACTS

Another great South American liberator was José de San Martin (1778–1850), the national hero of Argentina. He formed and trained his own forces, the Army of the Andes, and led them from Argentina across the Andes to defeat the Spanish at Cacubuco in 1817 and at Maipo in 1818. These victories liberated Chile.

———— ❑ ————

In 1821, San Martin proclaimed the liberation of Peru, but resigned as its protector in 1822, after differences with Bolívar.

———— ❑ ————

In 1826, Bolívar drew up the constitution of Bolivia, based on European styles of government. It became an important model for other South American states.

———— ❑ ————

The Congress of Panama, held in 1826, was the first international conference.

———— ❑ ————

The ideas of the French philosopher, Jean-Jacques Rousseau, inspired not only Bolívar, but also Maximilien Robespierre, the French revolutionary leader who established the Reign of Terror.

independent again by establishing the Second Venezuelan Republic.

In 1817, Bolívar and his rebels won the Battle of Boyaca. This victory liberated the colony of New Granada which was renamed Colombia. Bolívar then freed the rest of Venezuela and Ecuador and organized a federation or union of the three independent states. He became president of the federation which was named Gran Colombia.

Final victory

By 1823, Bolívar was also ruler of Peru. Victory against the Spaniards in the Battle of Ayacucho in 1824 finally freed South America from Spanish rule. In 1825, Upper Peru became a separate state, which was named Bolivia after the great liberator.

Bolívar dreamed of a united republic made up of the states he had liberated, but it was not to be. It was difficult to keep the newly independent states under control. One by one, they broke away from Gran Colombia until Bolívar only ruled Colombia itself. He resigned as her president in 1830.

Bolívar died in the same year, disillusioned by the loss of his united nation. However, the man known as the Liberator had a lasting influence on South America. Although he had not managed to hold his republic together, his ideas about government had a long-lasting effect and helped to shape the future of the new states.

Bolívar did not liberate South America alone, but his military skill and vision of western-style democracy helped to shape the continent as it emerged from Spanish domination.

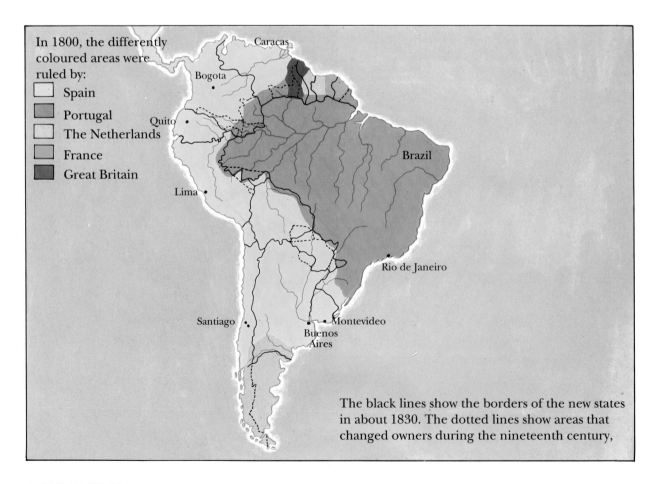

In 1800, the differently coloured areas were ruled by:

- Spain
- Portugal
- The Netherlands
- France
- Great Britain

Caracas
Bogota
Quito
Lima
Brazil
Rio de Janeiro
Santiago
Montevideo
Buenos Aires

The black lines show the borders of the new states in about 1830. The dotted lines show areas that changed owners during the nineteenth century.

Emperor Meiji opens up Japan

The Shogun of Japan gloomily read the report from Osaka Bay.
The 'foreign devils' had returned in their enormous ships and were
demanding to know if they could trade with Japan.
If he said yes, life in Japan would never be the same again. If he said no,
those warships were more powerful than anything at his command....

400	BC/AD	400	800	1200	1600	2000

1854 Tokyo, Japan

Today, Japan is a major industrial power. It is hard to believe that only 150 years ago, it was completely isolated from the rest of the world. Why was this and what happened to change things?

Japan had had emperors since about 660 BC, but from the twelfth century, onwards the country was ruled by the *shogun*. This was a military title which was passed from father to son. Tokugawa Ieyasu became *shogun* in 1603, and his family controlled Japan for two centuries.

Great power
Tokugawa Ieyasu organized the country into large estates under the control of lords known as *daimyos*. This system, in which the lords owed allegiance (loyalty) to the *shogun*, gave the Tokugawa *shoguns* great power.

Tokugawa Iemitsu, who came to power in 1622, tightened the family's control. He was afraid of losing Japan to the rule of a foreign country, so he stopped most foreign trade. Some trade with the Chinese and the Dutch was allowed, but Dutch traders had to stay on a small island off the Japanese city of Nagasaki. Japan was now virtually closed to the outside world.

Mutsuhito (1852–1912), Emperor Meiji of Japan, ended centuries of feudal rule, returned full power to the throne and encouraged Japan's modernization.

Tension and rebellion
The situation began to change in the nineteenth century. The *shoguns* were finding it difficult to maintain their control over the people. The nobles lived in luxury while the peasants who worked for them had very little. This caused resentment which often led to rebellion.

Also the merchants, who had always been near the bottom of the Japanese class system, were becoming more powerful. They had grown rich from trading at home, particularly from buying and selling rice. Now they wanted to open up foreign trade and increase their riches. Russia and Britain were both interested in trading with Japan. But it was the USA who finally persuaded the Japanese to open their ports to foreign trade.

Better relations

The US government had several reasons for wanting better relations with Japan. It was already trading with China, which brought it close to Japanese shores. Many American whaling ships sailed into the Pacific Ocean, so shipwrecked sailors were often washed up on Japanese beaches. The Japanese were hostile to these intruders on their isolated shores. The USA also wanted to be the first to profit from the new market.

In 1853, the USA decided to take action. President Millard Fillmore (1800–74) sent a squadron of ships to Japan, under the command of Commodore Matthew Perry . His orders were to deliver a letter from the president, asking the Japanese to treat shipwreck victims well and outlining a trading agreement between Japan and the USA.

The isolation ends

Perry arrived with four warships in Osaka Bay on 8 July 1953. His orders were to deliver the president's letter to the *shogun* and then leave. The Americans would return in a year's time for the Japanese reply.

Perry returned in 1854 with more ships, determined to get a treaty. The Japanese knew that they could not put up much resistance to the US navy,

FASCINATING FACTS

The word shogun *is the shortened form of an ancient military title which means 'supreme commander for the conquering of the barbarians'.· The first shogun was Minamoto Yoritomo, who was given the title by the emperor in 1192 after defeating the rival Taira clan.*

Commodore Matthew Perry (1794– 1858).

The daimyos *(nobles) lived in magnificent castles with massive fortifications to protect them from attack. These castles can still be seen in Japan. Relatives of the shoguns held the main cities and military sites. The rest of Japan was carved up into large estates for the other lords.*

———— ❑ ————

Tokugawa Iemitsu was so afraid of losing his grip on his people that he ruled that ships must be open and be no more than 22.8 metres long. He felt that no one would dare venture out to sea in such flimsy boats. The Japanese were amazed when Perry arrived with his warships, two of which were driven by steam.

———— ❑ ————

Japanese people travelled to the West to learn new skills. Skilled people came to Japan to help with the building of railways and ships. By the 1870s, the Japanese had even begun to dress like westerners.

and in March they signed the Treaty of Kanazawa, agreeing to the US proposals. The USA could now trade through the ports of Hakodate and Shimoda – both were far from Tokyo.

Other countries followed the USA's lead. By 1858, Britain, France, the Netherlands and Russia had all signed trade agreements with Japan.

Trend of change

The opening of Japan's ports began a trend of change and modernization which finally made Japan into one of the most successful industrial nations in the world. But there were still problems to come and Western ships met with resistance during the first few years of the agreements.

The next turning point was in 1867, when the Emperor Meiji came to the throne. During his forty-five year reign, Japan was transformed into a modern nation. Harbours and docks were extended and modernized to make way for foreign shipping, and banks and post offices were set up to make trading more efficient.

Japanese society also changed. Gone were the rich lords, the *samurai* and the poor peasants. Education improved and a professional, university-educated class emerged. The government put money into Japanese industries so that they could produce their own goods instead of importing them. These industries grew rapidly and, by 1900, the country, which had been so isolated, was a major world power.

The US Navy ships waited in Osaka Bay in 1854 while the treaty between the USA and Japan was discussed. The American sailors could see the Japanese open-decked boats which were used for trade within the country.

Palmerston & the Indian Mutiny

The rumour ran round the barracks like wildfire. "These new cartridges, the ones we have to bite open, they are covered in cow fat!"
This insult to the animal held sacred by Hindus was too much for the native soldiers. They killed their European officers and called on all Hindus to support them in throwing the British out of India once and for all.

400	BC/AD	400	800	1200	1600	2000

1856 Meerut, India

By the middle of the eighteenth century, India was dominated by the British East India Company, which had been set up in 1600 to trade in spices. At first, the company did not try to change the Indian way of life, but in the nineteenth century, ambitious British administrators began to have other ideas. They wanted to westernize India by converting the people to Christianity and by introducing western-style education. The administrators also set about modernizing India. Railways and telegraph systems were set up to improve communications.

Resentment and anger
The Indian people resented these changes. The princes who ruled over different states felt that their authority was being threatened. Some wealthy landowners had to sell their properties to pay taxes imposed by the British. Anger against the British was building up to a dangerous level.

The administrators and traders formed a fairly small part of the East India Company. By far the largest section was the army.

As the Company fought to gain more territories in India, they recruited Indians to boost their numbers, until there were about three times as many Indians as there were Europeans in the army. Many of these were Hindus who resented having to serve under British officers. In this

Viscount Palmerston (1784–1865), British foreign secretary and later Prime Minister, was the statesman responsible for making the British monarch, Victoria, ruler of India.

In 1857, the Indian rebels took the British by surprise when they poured into cities such as Delhi and Lucknow. The rebels were supported by the locals and so outnumbered the British. But extra troops were sent in and the British reclaimed India in 1858.

Queen Victoria (1819–1901) became Empress of India.

atmosphere it would not take much to spark off rebellion.

Trouble flared in 1857 when some Indian soldiers were imprisoned for disobeying orders. Three regiments of *sepoys* (Indian soldiers) broke into the jail and set them free. The rebel army then marched on Delhi.

The British were outnumbered by the rebels and their supporters who captured Delhi and moved on to besiege other cities, such as Lucknow.

There was near panic in Britain as the news filtered through, but Palmerston kept his head and sent extra troops from England. When they arrived, the army moved in to recapture Delhi. In 1858, they relieved Lucknow which had been under continuous siege. Fighting went on throughout the year, but many parts of India did not support the Mutiny. By the end of 1858, the British felt that they controlled India again.

Empress of India
However, the Mutiny had changed things for ever. In 1858, the British government passed the Government of India Act which took control of India away from the East India Company and gave it to the British Crown. Queen Victoria became the ruler of India. Later, in 1876, she became the Empress of India.

The attitude of the British in India also changed. They realized that they could no longer rely on Indian troops to protect British interests in India. However, Western education continued and many people still seemed to welcome British influence. But the events of the Mutiny were to lead to future unrest and eventually to India's independence.

Bismarck & German Unity

*In 1815, when the lands conquered by Napolean regained their freedom,
Germany was divided into more than twenty independent states.
During the nineteenth century, they slowly came together until, in 1871,
the King of Prussia became the Kaiser (Emperor) of Germany. This grand
confederation was masterminded by one political genius – Bismarck.*

400	BC/AD	400	800	1200	1600	2000

1871 Berlin, Germany

At the beginning of the nineteenth century, Germany was divided into separate states – many of them very small. However, there was a growing feeling that Germany should be one united country, but people were divided about the form it should take.

One group wanted a huge country made up of all the German-speaking states, which would be dominated by the Austrian Empire. Another preferred a smaller Germany which would be dominated by the northern kingdom of Prussia and would not include Austria.

Bitter rivals

Austria and Prussia remained bitter rivals for many years. But Prussia's industry was growing in strength. The growing railway network linked it with the other states, and it had large coal and oil industries.

In 1834, a customs union (called the *Zollverein*) of eighteen states was formed. This customs union, which was dominated by Prussia, established trade links between the member states. Austria was not included.

Forging a united Germany

Then in 1858, Wilhelm I (1797–1888) of Prussia declared that he wanted to unite Germany under Prussian leadership. He knew that this would be unpopular with many people, so he appointed Bismarck as chancellor (head of government), to help him.

The 'Iron Chancellor', as Bismarck came to be known, quickly exerted his power. In 1864, he led a war against Denmark to bring the provinces of Schleswig and Holstein under German control. In 1866, the rivalry between Prussia and Austria led to a war which

The 'Iron Chancellor', Prince Otto Leopold von Bismarck (1815–98). Under his leadership, Prussia defeated Austria and France, and Germany was united.

the Prussians won easily. The next year, Bismarck formed the new North German Confederation, which united the states of Westphalia, Alsace-Lorraine, Schleswig and Holstein under Prussian leadership.

The Confederation expands

Prussia was still maintaining its economic dominance. As well as its trade links through the *Zollverein*, Bismarck built up trade with England, Belgium, Italy and France, but Austria was still excluded. The southern states saw that there were financial advantages in joining Prussia, and they became part of the Confederation.

There had been a series of wars with France and the Prussians had suffered a humiliating defeat by Napoleon I in 1806. Bismarck thought that one more war with France would finally unite the northern and southern states. In 1870, he provoked Emperor Napoleon III (1808–73) to declare a war which the Germans won. Bismarck had been careful to ensure that Prussia stayed powerful enough to dominate a united Germany. Finally, in March 1871, the king of Prussia was crowned kaiser (emperor) of a united Germany.

Bismarck stayed as chancellor of Germany until 1890. He made sure that Germany kept up good relations with other countries. Industries produced more products. Merchants began to travel the world, increasing trade and Germany's wealth. Bismarck had created a major world power.

Bismarck had the strength and ruthlessness to bring the many separate states of Germany together under one emperor, using force or negotiation as required to achieve his ends.

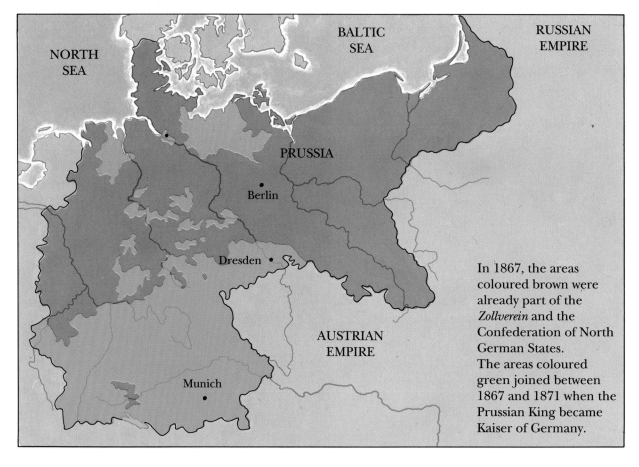

In 1867, the areas coloured brown were already part of the *Zollverein* and the Confederation of North German States.
The areas coloured green joined between 1867 and 1871 when the Prussian King became Kaiser of Germany.

Lenin & the Russian Revolution

In April 1917, a sealed train rattled across Europe from Switzerland to St Petersburg. It was carrying a Russian exile to meet his destiny. Within six months, he was in control of the vast Russian Empire, commanding a revolution that would uproot people from the Baltic to the Bering Straits and inspire many others to revolt elsewhere.

400	BC/AD	400	800	1200	1600	2000

1918 St Petersberg, Russia

In 1917, there was a revolution in Russia which ended nearly 400 years of rule by powerful tsars or emperors. Life was grim for ordinary Russian people. The peasants who farmed the land found it difficult to survive because they were taxed heavily, and they also had to pay high rents to the landlords who owned the farms. Russian factories were old-fashioned and factory workers were forced to accept very low wages. There was a shortage of housing, and people had to live in badly overcrowded conditions.

Ready to fight

This situation made the working people very unhappy, and many were ready to fight for better conditions.

In 1904, war broke out with Japan and, to everyone's surprise, Japan defeated the Russian army and nearly destroyed the naval fleet.

Vladimir Ilyich Lenin (1870–1924) led the Bolshevik faction during the Russian revolution. He had spent ten years in exile in Switzerland, before returning in April 1917.

The humiliation of this defeat increased the unrest in Russia.

Fighting in the streets

The situation was made worse in 1905 when a group of demonstrators marching to present a petition – a message from the people – to Tsar Nicholas II (1868–1918) were shot down by troops in St Petersburg. Nearly half a million workers went on strike, and there was fighting in the streets. In the countryside, peasants revolted against their landlords and a peasants' union was set up to fight for better conditions. Workers in factories in St Petersburg set up the first 'soviets' or workers' councils.

But, in December 1905, a new government was formed. It included a few of the leaders who were in favour of change. The revolution was over for the moment. There were good harvests for a few years, and industrial production increased. But working conditions were still poor.

The unrest erupted again in 1912. There were over 2,000 factory strikes in that year, and more than 3,000 strikes in the first six months of 1914. There were also demonstrations against the tsar.

Events elsewhere in Europe took over from problems at home later that year, when Russia entered the First World War against Germany. But the war made the workers' situation worse than ever. Industries began to produce equipment for the army instead of the tools the farmers needed.

Government money was poured into the armed forces. Factory owners were becoming rich by making army equipment, but none of this wealth was passed on to the workers. There were food shortages and prices rose. Soon the strikes began again.

October revolution

By 1917, even the army was joining the demonstrations against the government. In March, the tsar was forced to give up the throne and a new government, led by Kerensky and the Mensheviks, was formed.

The new government managed to hold power for eight months, but they wanted to protect middle-class interests. However, the workers wanted a government which would support them, allowing peasants to own land and giving more power to factory workers. The main party behind these proposed reforms were the Bolsheviks, led by Vladimir Ilyich Lenin. The Bolsheviks also wanted factories and banks to be owned by the state instead of by individual owners.

During 1917, the Bolsheviks became

more and more popular with the factory workers. Kerensky's government tried to use the army to rule the country, but this only made the people support the Bolsheviks more strongly. By September, the Bolsheviks were the dominant force in most of the soviets.

Lenin wanted to seize power from the government immediately, but he was persuaded to wait a while. Kerensky was beginning to lose his power and the government was failing. Waiting for the right moment would make it all the easier to take over.

Bolsheviks take power

Meanwhile, there was rioting and unrest among peasants and workers. The army could not stop these revolts and, at the end of September, the Bolsheviks decided that it was time for action. A headquarters was set up in the capital, St Petersburg, which had been renamed Petrograd. The Bolsheviks took over telegraph and postal networks and railway stations, stopping food supplies to the city.

The government met in the Winter Palace, the former home of the tsars, to decide what to do. But there were few government ministers left and they had no hope against the revolutionaries. When the Bolsheviks attacked the palace, the government ministers surrendered without a fight.

So the Bolsheviks took power and Lenin began to put his reforms into practice. He wanted a system of workers' control in the factories, and

It was not difficult for the Bolsheviks to storm the Winter Palace in October 1917.
But the attack was an important symbol that the workers' revolution had succeeded.

he thought that land should become the property of the 'entire people'. A Bolshevik government was formed, and it immediately called for an end to the war. Industries were nationalized and worker control of factories began.

Civil war

The Bolsheviks thought that now industry would prosper, but they had under-estimated the damage done by the years of unrest and an expensive war. In fact, industrial production dropped further. Unemployment and food shortages followed. The peasants were a little better off because they no longer had to pay rent for their land to landlords. But there was not enough land to farm, and there was still a desperate shortage of equipment.

The Bolsheviks, which later became the Communist Party, revised some of their policies, but there was opposition from anti-communist 'White' Russians and in 1918 civil war broke out. The 'Red' Communists won in 1920, but not before thousands had been killed.

By then, the Communist Party had got a firm grip on the country which it maintained until the 1990s.

Unrest among the ordinary people of Russia led to the downfall of the last tsar, Nicholas II.

Gandhi & Indian Independence

'We cannot fight the British,' said Gandhi over and over to the firebrands of the Indian National Congress. 'We must find another way to gain independence – an Indian way.' So he formulated his campaigns of disobedience, embarrassing the government, but not provoking them. In the end, he won independence for India.

400	BC/AD	400	800	1200	1600	2000

1930 Dandi, India

British rule in India had caused unrest since the days of the Indian Mutiny (1857–8). In 1885, the Indian National Congress was formed to fight for Indian rights and a say in how the country was run. But very little changed until a new nationalist leader emerged during the First World War. His name was Mohandâs Karamchand Gandhi, who became known as *Mahatma*, which means 'Great Soul'.

General strikes

Gandhi became the leader of the Indian National Congress in 1914. He urged his followers to begin a series of general strikes against British rule. Then, in 1919, British troops opened fire at a mass street-meeting, and 379 Indians were killed.

Gandhi now changed his policies. He believed that India must rid itself of British rule altogether,

Mohandâs Karamchand Gandhi (1869–1948) was born in India and went to England in 1888 to study law. He practised law in South Africa before returning to India in 1914.

but he knew this could not be achieved by fighting. So he pioneered policies of peaceful resistance to the British government in India. One of these was his policy of non-co-operation, which meant that the Indian people would refuse to obey the British authorities.

Religious conflict

However, Gandhi's plan did not work. A continual problem was fighting between the Hindus and Muslims – the two main religious groups in India – which made it difficult to unite the country.

Many parts of India also continued to co-operate with Britain, and the nationalist politicians who wanted India to be governed by Indians went back to negotiating with the government.

Gandhi was put in prison in 1922 for his policies and spent two

There were terrible riots between Muslims and Hindus during the run up to Indian independence and afterwards.

Gandhi's thin, frail figure was the opposite of military might. It symbolized the peaceful leadership he favoured. But his policy of civil disobedience, called satyagraha, did persuade the British to make some reforms in India.

In 1931, the leaders of Congress met the British Viceroy, Lord Irvin, and drew up an agreement called the Delhi Pact. This ended the civil disobedience campaign in return for government reforms leading towards independence. By 1935, it looked as though independence might be achieved peacefully, but this was thwarted by the start of World War II.

years in a British jail. When he was released, he withdrew from politics and travelled round India, campaigning to improve conditions for the people.

By 1929, the nationalist politicians had realized that the British were not going to give up their rule and that their negotiations were causing more unrest among the Indians. They were finding it impossible to keep the people happy and still stay on reasonable terms with the British.

Another Indian leader, Jawaharlal Nehru (1889–1964), was now speaking out for independence. He was elected president of the Indian National Congress in 1929, taking over from his father, Motilal Nehru. In 1930, Gandhi returned to launch a second campaign of non-co-operation. This time many more people supported him.

Gandhi's salt march

In the same year, Gandhi made his famous salt march as a protest against the government's salt tax. Everyone in India had to buy salt manufactured by the state even though they could make it much more cheaply themselves. So Gandhi walked 385 kilometres to the coast at Dandi, where he extracted salt from sea water.

At first, the government ignored Gandhi's protest, but thousands joined him on his march. 'We are marching in the name of God,' said Gandhi, and he instructed his followers to make salt themselves. Newspaper reporters from all over the world followed his progress. Local government officials along the way abandoned their jobs to join the Indian cause. Gandhi's salt march made a big impact, but both he and Nehru were imprisoned.

I want world sympathy in this battle of Right against Might.

Santi   MKGandhi
5.4.'30

*Nehru and Lord Mountbatten,
the last British Viceroy.*

FASCINATING FACTS

*Britain tried to hand power over to a united India in 1945, but these efforts failed because of protests from the Muslim League.
This league had been formed in 1906 to protect the interests of the Muslims as there were far more Hindus in India.*

———————— ❑ ————————

*Mohammed Ali Jinnah (1876–1948) was a member of the Muslim League and the Indian National Congress.
At first he tried to unite Hindus and Muslims, but he resigned from the Congress in 1930 because of Gandhi's policies.
Jinnah became president of the League in 1934 and began to work for a separate state for the Muslims.
He became the first governor-general of Pakistan.*

———————— ❑ ————————

The Muslim League insisted on 'partition', which meant creating two separate states before independence. More than a million people fled from Pakistan to India and from India to Pakistan between August and October 1947 to escape religious persecution.

Gandhi again withdrew from politics for much of the 1930s while the Congress continued to work towards independence. When the Second World War broke out in 1939, Gandhi was torn between Indian support for the British against Hitler and his own policy of non-violence. Co-operating with Britain in the war went against his policy for independence.

Independence for India

In 1942, the British offered India complete independence after the war if they would help Britain to win it. Gandhi replied that the British should leave India immediately. Gandhi and the other Congress leaders were jailed until 1944, when they were released to start discussions about independence.

Talks led to an agreed date for independence – 15 August 1947 – but a major problem was still the fighting between Hindus and Muslims. As a result, the separate state of Pakistan was created so that Muslims would have a state of their own.

Serious fighting broke out between the two religious groups in Bengal and elsewhere, so Gandhi began a fast as a protest. He hoped that his action would bring the two sides together. But his suggestions that Hindus and Muslims should be friends greatly angered a group of Hindu fanatics. On 30 January 1948, one of these Hindus shot Gandhi dead as he went to pray.

Gandhi was regarded as a supreme Indian leader for many years before his death, and he played an important part in achieving independence for his country. His method of peaceful resistance inspired thousands to follow him and aroused sympathy for his cause all over the world.

Mao & the Chinese Long March

Mao crashed his fist on the table to silence the argument. 'We cannot stay in Jiangxi,' he asserted, 'the blockade is getting tighter and tighter. We must break out and march to where the army can regroup.' 'Where can we go?' asked one officer. 'To Shaanxi province. We have friends there.' Silence followed – everyone knew Shaanxi was over 9,000 miles away....

400	BC/AD	400	800	1200	1600	2000

1935 Shansi Province, China

China became a republic in 1911 after the Qing (Manchu) dynasty had been overthrown. The nationalist party – the Kuomintang – formed a government in Canton, but there was a military government in Beijing and warlords ruled in the provinces. There was also a strong communist following and the Chinese Communist Party was formed in July 1921. One of its founders was Mao Zedong. It was the communists, under Mao, who would finally unite China.

Leaders executed
In 1925, the commander-in-chief of the nationalist army, Chiang Kai-shek, became leader of the Kuomintang. At first, Chiang made the communists his allies when his army fought the warlords and the military government in Beijing. They took control of several cities, including Nanjing and Shanghai. But Chiang later decided that the communists were becoming too powerful. He ordered the execution of their leaders in Shanghai and threw all the communist members out of his government.

A turning point came in 1927, when part of the nationalist army rebelled in support of the communists. The rebels banded together to form the communist Red Army.

The Red Army made several unsuccessful attempts to take towns and cities from the nationalists. One of these, the attempted take-over of Changsa, capital of the province of Hunan, was led by Mao Zedong.

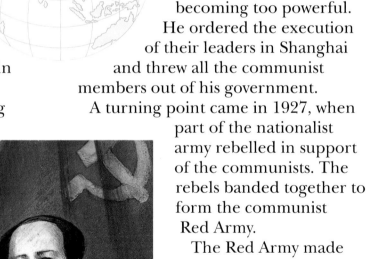

Mao Zedong or Tse-tung (1893–1976). His communists united China, and he was Chairman of the People's Republic of China in 1949–58 and 1966–76.

Winning support
Mao realized that taking cities was not the way to win power in China. The

answer lay with the people who lived in the countryside. There were tens of millions of peasants, and if they united in support of the communists, they could overcome the nationalists.

Mao also decided on different tactics for the Red Army. If the nationalists attacked, the Red Army would pretend to retreat, but would in fact regroup behind enemy lines. They could then cut off the nationalist army's escape routes and go on the attack with the help of the peasants. These new tactics were successful. Chiang's army began to lose campaigns, while the Red Army won more support.

A bad decision
In 1931, the communists won a victory at Kaoshing in Jiangxi province. Chiang had had to withdraw his troops to deal with the Japanese who had occupied Manchuria in northern China. This left Jiangxi under communist control. They set up their own government, the Chinese Soviet Republic, run along Russian lines.

The nationalists returned to the attack, but they could not take Jiangxi. So in 1933, Chiang decided to blockade Jiangxi by cutting off supplies of food and materials. The communists would not be able to survive for long under these conditions. About 700,000 nationalist troops blocked every route into the province and no supplies could get in.

Right. The marchers cross the flimsy bridge over the Tatu River. The long march was a retreat rather than a victory, but it made Mao famous as the leader of the Chinese Communist Party.

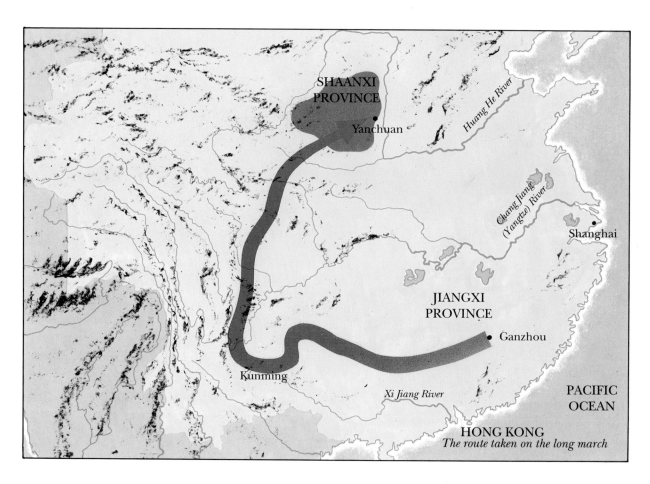

SHAANXI PROVINCE

Yanchuan

Huang He River

Chang Jiang (Yangtze) River

Shanghai

JIANGXI PROVINCE

Ganzhou

Kunming

Xi Jiang River

PACIFIC OCEAN

HONG KONG
The route taken on the long march

Mao and his followers encountered many dangers on the long march. One of these was the crossing of the Tatu River. This river had a bridge across a deep gorge. The bridge was made of chains with planks laid across them. The nationalists knew that the communists had to cross the river there so they removed the planks, but they could not unfasten the chains. Guards were left on the bridge to ambush the communists.

Twenty of Mao's followers swung along the chains, being fired at all the time. When they had overpowered the guards, the marchers replaced the planks and crossed the bridge.

During World War II, the rival nationalist and communist armies were forced to join forces against Japan, who had conquered a large part of northern China in 1931. But after the Japanese defeat in 1945, civil war broke out again.

———— ❏ ————

Between 1947 and 1949, when he communists defeated the Kuomintang, Chiang Kai-shek and about 2,000,000 of his supporters were forced to flee to Taiwan, a large island off the south-east coast of China. There he founded the Republic of China which consists of Taiwan and several nearby islands.

General Chiang Kai-shek (1887–1975).

But then some of the nationalist troops rebelled against their leaders and asked the communists for support. The communists turned them down.

This was a bad decision because the rebels could have provided supplies and the communists could have helped the revolution against the nationalists. By the summer of 1934, the communists realized that they could not go on. Mao had to make a desperate decision. They had to escape from Jiangxi, and so the famous long march began.

On the long march

The communists broke out of Jiangxi and marched over 9,600 kilometres to the soviet province of Shaanxi in the north-west. They marched about 50 kilometres a day, and sometimes more. There were hazards along the way and they had to travel through difficult countryside. They had to cross the Great Snow Mountains and the uninhabited swamps of eastern Tibet.

Nationalist troops waited everywhere to ambush them, but Mao and his comrades pushed on. Many of his followers did not survive the journey, but by October 1936, more supporters had joined Mao in Shaanxi. The Red Army numbered 80,000 men and was again a threat to Chiang Kai-shek.

It was many years before China was united under communist rule. But it is certain the communists would not have survived without the long march.

In 1939, Mao became Chairman of the Central Committee of the Communist Party. He continued to build up support for the party until he became Chairman of the communist People's Republic of China in 1949.

Eleanor Roosevelt & the U.N.

When Franklin D. Roosevelt died in 1945, the Allies knew that World War II was almost over. But world peace was a battle still to be won. Eleanor Roosevelt knew that the ordinary people, who had suffered so much, needed a champion to stand up for their rights. She fought first for refugees and then in writing the UN Charter to ensure they would not be forgotten.

400   BC/AD   400   800   1200   1600   2000

1945 San Francisco, California, USA

Throughout history, wars have been a way of solving power struggles and rivalries between different peoples and countries. For centuries, armies and navies have set out to conquer new lands or defend their own territory, often with great loss of life on both sides of the conflict.

In the two world wars in this century, millions of people were killed, while towns and cities were destroyed by bombing. Most people felt that such terrible wars should never happen again.

League of Nations fails

The problem was to find a peaceful yet successful way of settling problems and disputes between nations. The League of Nations was set up after the First World War with the aim of achieving world peace. It was successful at first, but during the 1930s it failed to deal with the events

Eleanor Roosevelt (1884–1962) acted as her husband's political representative when he was ill with polio. This experience was to prove valuable in later years.

which led to the Second World War.

After World War II, people were even more determined that peaceful solutions must be found for disputes between countries. So, in October 1945, the United Nations (or UN) was formed to promote world peace. Its aims were to prevent war, to foster good relations and settle grievances between nations, and to work for human rights and freedoms for all.

Peacekeeping duties

It was decided that the five nations who had been victors in the war should be responsible for keeping world peace. These nations – the USA, China, the USSR, Great Britain and France – would combine to provide peacekeeping forces in the world's troublespots.

However, they were not the only members of the

UN. In all, fifty-one nations became founding members and that number was to increase as time went by.

The beginning of a dream

Two world leaders were planning the formation of the UN while the war was still raging. They were the then President of the USA, Franklin D. Roosevelt (1882–1945), and the Prime Minister of Great Britain, Winston Churchill (1874–1965). However, a few weeks before the end of the war, Roosevelt died suddenly. It was his widow, Eleanor, who was to prove an important influence in the future work of the UN.

Past US presidents' wives had remained in the background, but not Eleanor Roosevelt. She had spoken out in her own right about racial inequality and the plight of the poor. In 1945, President Harry S. Truman (1884–1972) asked Eleanor to serve as US delegate at the first meeting of the UN in London. At the meeting, she was given a job on Committee III, which would deal with humanitarian, social and cultural problems.

Refugee issue

In 1946, Committee III had to tackle a very serious issue. The war had left over a million people in refugee camps

The nations that were most influential in the setting up of the UN were the USSR, the USA and Great Britain (represented here by Joseph Stalin (1879–1953), Roosevelt and Churchill – the leaders of the three countries during World War II). These three nations, with France and China, are the permanent members of the Security Council of the UN. This is the body that has the greatest responsibility for maintaining peace throughout the world.

The General Assembly is in New York; each member nation has one vote.

UNICEF provides health care and education, mostly in the Third World.

FAO helps people to farm and eat better, and watches over famine areas.

in Europe. Their homelands were countries like Poland and Hungary, which were now occupied by the Russians. The Russians demanded that the refugees should be sent home, but the refugees did not want to live under communist rule.

Eleanor made a rousing speech in which she argued that forcing these people to return would breach their rights as human beings with freedom of choice. Her speech won the day and the Russians lost their case.

Defining human rights
Eleanor's speech was so successful that she was asked to be the US delegate on a UN commission to prepare a 'Declaration of Human Rights'. The members of the commission came from all over the world, and the task of discussing and analysing what every country wanted was enormous. The other members of the commission chose Eleanor to be their chairwoman. It is largely due to her work that the Declaration appeared at all and that it was adopted by the UN in 1948.

A world organization
The original idea of the UN was that member nations should genuinely wish for peace. As time went by, it became clear that the UN could not act unless

UNESCO promotes education, science and cultural exchanges.

The UNHCR helps refugees with emergency and long-term aid.

There are more than twelve large UN peacekeeping forces in action today.

The World Health Organization (WHO)
fights disease around the world.

just about every nation was a member, whether they were peace-loving or not. Many more nations were admitted in 1955, and today it is a world organization with 178 members.

Its formation was a turning point in looking for peaceful solutions to disputes, but it has not been entirely successful. Wars have not always been avoided and human rights continue to be abused in the world. There have been criticisms about international trading agreements and the gap between rich and poor nations. Yet the UN is the only way in which nations of the world can unite to try and put an end to injustices and atrocities.

The UN emblem is recognized
all over the world.

FASCINATING FACTS

The United Nations was formed on 24 October 1945 (United Nations Day).
Its headquarters is in New York, USA.
There were a total of fifty-one founding members of the organization and the original idea for membership was that each nation should honour the charter, which stressed that members should be 'peace-loving'.

———□———

The UN has done much valuable work since it was formed, particularly through its specialist agencies. The World Health Organization (WHO), the Children's Fund (UNICEF), the Food and Agricultural Organization (FAO), the United Nations Educational, Scientific and Cultural Organization (UNESCO) and the United Nations High Commissioner for Refugees (UNHCR) provide medical help, food distribution, aid for people devastated by natural disasters, and help for children and refugees from wars.

———□———

Eleanor Roosevelt believed that:
'If civilization is to survive, we must cultivate the science of human relationships – the ability of all people of all kinds to live together and work together in the same world, at peace.'

———□———

The UN is still dominated by the five nations who form the Security Council. This makes it difficult for the UN to act in conflicts involving one of these nations. The General Assembly is the main debating body of the UN, and has a representative from each member nation. But each member has only one vote, even though some countries have far larger populations than others.

———□———

The Declaration of Human Rights said that everyone is born equal and sets out the rights of every person in every aspect of life, from religion and ownership of property, to education and the right to a fair trial.
One article said that no one should be tortured or made to suffer degrading punishments. But some governments have failed to abide by it, and inequality, torture and bloodshed are still common in many parts of the world.

Gorbachev & the Berlin Wall

"An iron curtain has been drawn across Europe," said Winston Churchill in 1946, as communists snatched power across Eastern Europe. The most blatant sign of that division was the massive wall that divided Berlin into two cities. When the Berlin Wall was breached on 8 November 1989, the world knew that a new era had begun.

400	BC/AD	400	800	1200	1600	2000

1989 Berlin, Germany

Despite the setting up of the UN, the alliance between some of the major powers soon became uneasy. During World War II, Poland Czechoslovakia and Hungary had been occupied by Germany, while Romania had given military support to Germany's leader, Adolf Hitler. By the end of the war, the Russians had moved into most of central and eastern Europe. Germans and supporters of Hitler were expelled, and communist governments set up in these countries.

Communism spreads

Germany itself was occupied by the allied forces of Britain, France, the USA and the USSR. The area occupied by the USSR became the German Democratic Republic, also known as East Germany.

The communists used great skill in persuading the people that their way

Mikhail Gorbachev (1931–) is the son of a farmer. After excelling at school, he studied law at Moscow State University, and became the last USSR president in 1988.

was best. Two or three years after the war had ended, all the countries in what came to be known as the 'eastern bloc' were single-party communist states. This meant that there was no other sort of political party to oppose them. The communist party could impose anything on the people.

The 'iron curtain'

In 1946, Winston Churchill said that an 'iron curtain' was being drawn across Europe. Europe was divided into two parts, and the communist countries were referred to as being 'behind the iron curtain'. Although the USSR was one of the nations on the UN Security Council, there was a strained relationship between East and West.

The Cold War, as this situation came to be known, lasted until 1989. Then, seemingly overnight, everything changed. These changes were largely brought about by one man, Mikhail Gorbachev, who became the Soviet leader in 1985. His policies of openness (*glasnost*) and re-structuring (*perestroika*) freed the USSR from the threat of military rule and allowed the nations of Eastern Europe to take their freedom back.

No demonstrations allowed

From the start of the communist take-over in 1945, there were protests about the system. People wanted reforms which would give them more freedom of choice. These protests often took the form of demonstrations, which were suppressed instantly – and often violently – by the communists.

In 1953, there were demonstrations in East Germany against poverty and the loss of freedom. The Soviet troops crushed the riots by firing shots at the demonstrators. The centre of the rioting was in the city of Berlin.

In 1948, Berlin had been divided into two – East Berlin, occupied by the Russians, and West Berlin, which was shared between the three Western allies. After the riots in East Berlin, a steady flow of refugees began to cross the border into West Berlin.

So, in 1961, the East German government and the Russians built the Berlin Wall to divide the city. This wall was heavily guarded, and anyone who tried to cross it to the West was shot.

There were similar protests in other parts of the Eastern bloc. In 1956 in Hungary, and in 1968 in Czechoslovakia, leaders tried to introduce reforms which would give the people more freedom. These were both brutally suppressed by Soviet invasions.

FASCINATING FACTS

In October 1989, Mikhail Gorbachev visited East Berlin and told the East German leaders that Moscow would not help to keep them in power.

On 3 December 1989, the US president, George Bush, and Mikhail Gorbachev formally announced the end of the Cold War.

In January 1990, the non-Russian republics of the Soviet Union began to press for independence. In February, Gorbachev announced that the Communist Party would give up its right to rule.

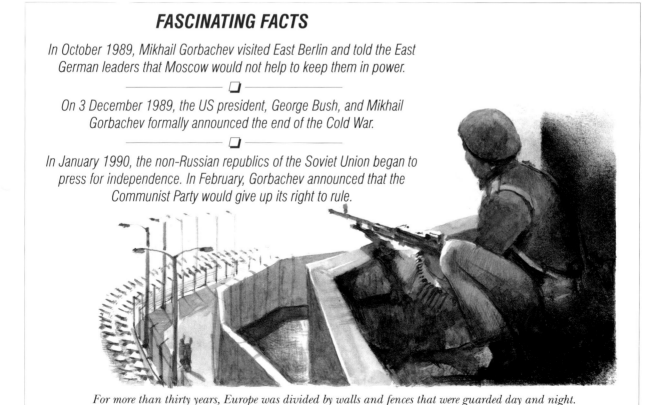

For more than thirty years, Europe was divided by walls and fences that were guarded day and night.

In 1980, strikes and demonstrations against the government in Poland had led to a change of leadership. But the situation worsened, bringing about the rise of the independent trade union, Solidarity, led by Lech Walesa (1943–). In 1981, Solidarity was accused of trying to overthrow the government and its leaders were arrested.

The situation between East and West began to change during the 1960s and 1970s. Relations between Bonn, the capital of West Germany, and Moscow improved. The USA and Western Europe also improved their relations with the USSR, although both sides were armed with nuclear weapons. During the 1980s, after very lengthy talks between the USA and USSR, both sides agreed to reduce the number of nuclear weapons they held.

The end of the Cold War
Despite this thaw in the Cold War, everyone was amazed at how quickly and dramatically changes came about after Mikhail Gorbachev became the Soviet party leader in 1985. Discussion between the Soviets and the Western powers began.

As an atmosphere of greater freedom grew, some of the eastern countries began to break away from total communism and introduce more western ideas. In 1988, the communist party leader in Hungary was replaced by a new leader, who was willing to see major reforms.

In Poland, discussions between the Polish leader, General Wojciech

This slogan on the Berlin Wall says 'Live alone and free, like a tree, but in the brotherhood of the forest'. The breaking-down of the wall gave East Germans this freedom.

N UND FREI, WIE EIN BAYER UM

RLICH WIE EIN WALD

The lives of many Europeans have changed dramatically since the magical night of 9 November 1989 when the Berlin Wall was first breached. Eastern bloc countries are queueing up to joining the European Union and NATO. On the downside, the problems in what was Yugoslavia are causing great tension throughout Europe.

Jaruzelski (1923–), and Solidarity led to the election of the first non-communist leader of an eastern-bloc state.

By 1989, large numbers of East Germans began to leave their country in search of a better life in West Germany. They travelled through Hungary, Czechoslovakia and the West German embassy in Warsaw, capital of Poland. Unable to stop the mass emigrations, the East German government resigned on 7 November. On 9 November, protesters made the first hole in the Berlin Wall.

Germany reunited

As more and more gaps were hacked in the concrete barrier, people from East Berlin flooded out into the West. The East German communist leaders were desperate to find a way of hanging on to power, but their attempts at reform failed and a new government was elected. In October 1990, West and East Germany became one country again. There would be many problems to come as the two sides tried to sort out their very different ways of life, but the people of East Germany were free.

There were revolutions in other central and eastern European countries at the end of 1989. In Czechoslovakia, the communist regime was replaced quite peacefully, but Romania suffered a long and bloody conflict to remove its leader, Nicolae Ceausescu (1918–89).

The lives of many Europeans have been transformed since 1989. There are still great changes to be made and problems to be solved. It will be many years before we can see the full results of these dramatic events that, quite literally, changed the world.

Find Out Some More

Museums and Other Places to Visit

There are many museums that have exhibits on the ancient world and events in history – find out from your library if there is one near you. If you can, try to visit one of the following museums:

The *British Museum* has galleries devoted to Greek, Roman, Egyptian Western Asiatic, Oriental, Japanese and Medieval periods. In addition, the museum has historical manuscripts on display, including the Magna Carta. Its address is: Great Russel Street, London WC1B 3DG. Telephone: 071–636 5555.

The *Victoria and Albert Museum* has galleries devoted to China, Japan, India and the Middle East. Its address is: Cromwell Road, South Kensington, London SW7 2RL. Telephone: 071–938 8500.

English Heritage has information on historic monuments and ruins that you can visit. For example, you can visit Lullingstone Roman Villa in Kent, or Hadrian's Wall, which for 250 years stood as Rome's northern frontier.

For further information, contact English Heritage, Keysign House, 429 Oxford Street, London W1R 2HD. Telephone: 071–973 5000.

Books to Read

Absolute Rulers by Michael Pollard (Heinemann, 1991)
The Ancient Chinese by Hazel Mary Martell (Heinemann, 1992)
China: A New Revolution? by John Bradley (Watts/Gloucester, 1990)
China Since 1945 by Stuart Ross (Wayland, 1988)
Conquerors by Nigel Grant (Macdonald, 1981)
The Expeditions of Cortes by Nigel Hunter (Wayland, 1990)
The French Revolution and Napoleon by Stephen Pratt (Wayland, 1992)
Gandhi by Nigel Hunter (Wayland, 1986)
Glasnost and Perestroika by Nigel Hawkes (Wayland, 1990)
The Russian Revolution by Stuart Ross (Wayland, 1988)
Spotlight on the Age of Revolution by Michael Gibson (Wayland, 1985)
Spotlight on the British Raj by William Golant (Wayland, 1988)
Twenty Tyrants by Alan Blackwood (Wayland, 1989)

Index